FORWARD AGGRESSIVE AND LIVING OUT LOUD

Self-Defense to Protect and Power Your Life

RICK MIRANDETTE

LifeRich Publishing is a registered trademark of The Reader's Digest Association, Inc.

LifeRich Publishing books may be ordered through booksellers or by contacting:

LifeRich Publishing
1663 Liberty Drive
Bloomington, IN 47403
www.liferichpublishing.com
844-686-9607

Illustrations: Ross McCrory and Josh Workman
Editing: Roslyn Mirandette

ISBN: 978-1-4897-3785-4 (sc)
ISBN: 978-1-4897-3784-7 (hc)
ISBN: 978-1-4897-3794-6 (e)

Library of Congress Control Number: 2021945956

Print information available on the last page.

LifeRich Publishing rev. date: 02/19/2022

DEDICATION

This book is dedicated to my three sons, who, accepting that life can be a struggle, even with its beauty, and wonder.........struggle well. Erik, honorable, powerful and committed. He takes the high road persevering with a boundless hopeful heart, managing challenges and risks to live his best life with love and adventure. Jake, a man of high ideals, a solid work ethic, creativity and endless optimism. His infectious energy and sense of humor ignites the whole room. There's nothing he can't accomplish. And to Alex, who exemplified strength, integrity, and a loving tender heart. A better man, I have never met nor been. His light, that we had for 18 years, is forever missed.

CONTENTS

ACKNOWLEDGMENTS

I want to thank the many instructors and friends who contributed to my martial arts, military and law enforcement knowledge. To the endless hours we spent training, refining and challenging techniques while having fun on and off the mats.

Thanks to all the survivors. Those who have experienced and survived trauma; who shared their stories to help others avoid trauma and live larger. They are all heroes in my book.

I want to thank my wife for her many hours of proofreading. She is good at spotting things I miss. To my friend, Ross McCrory, for his dedication, time and expert illustration rendering. To my son Jake and his friend who posed for those illustrations.

Thanks to all the warriors of the past who passed on the best of their art; who didn't do it just for sport, fitness or fun but for real—to survive. And thanks to all those who feel called to be the sheepdogs, and the thin blue line, for their willingness, courage and sacrifices in protecting others.

Thanks to the students, you, who read, digest and invest in the concept of being your own life guard; those who wish to stand strong for their rights, life and mission.

Rick Mirandette

Grand Master of Martial Arts (8th degree), Personal Protection Specialist

PREFACE

I've always been a person who wants to share the good things that I come across whether that be to notice a sunset or give away a good recipe, share great music or a well-crafted phrase that inspires. I get a little joy from bringing that richness or value to others. The knowledge of self-defense, how to be your own bodyguard, that helps shape ones confidence and courage, is one of those things.

Growing up, I was small for my age. Starting kindergarten before my 5th birthday didn't help. I was no stranger to being picked on. Today it's called bullying. I remember wishing for a superpower as if that were really possible. How does a smaller person have a chance against the superior force of the big kid? Trying to choke down cooked spinach wasn't pleasant but hey, it worked for Popeye. His battleship tattooed biceps came to life and he was able to easily trounce the bigger, meaner Bluto (later Brutus). What was the answer? Is it possible for a smaller, weaker person to survive in a world of giants? No one wants to feel insecure or intimidated and, some childhood fears can carry over to adulthood which just might hamper our successes. Not good. I remember a good friend of mine, who I wished was *my* girlfriend at the time, I was 15 or so, told me that her boyfriend was physically abusive. Wow…. I wanted to help but how? What could I say? What could she do?

As I got older, I learned that it wasn't a superpower or a food group that would enable an effective countermeasure to a larger imposing force. It was knowledge, tactics and strategy combined with discipline and training. It's knowing how to improve and refine our strengths and leverage them against the adversary's weaknesses. For instance: Knowing how to use postures and positioning helps mitigate an effective assault and puts you in an advantageous position for your countermeasures. And did you know that increasing the speed of your punch or kick increases the force? (Einstein's $E=mc^2$) Not to mention making it blindingly fast. I learned about force multipliers and a little about the art of war and now, after a lifetime of discovery and teaching these techniques to students, I decided to bring this information to you in a book.

I have been teaching martial arts, self-defense and fitness for 45 years. My interest and curiosity in the arts, sparked by Hollywood movies showing superhuman feats of fighting ability, took me to many dojos (Japanese for martial arts school), seminars, competitions and special training classes both in the U.S. and abroad. I studied a few styles whole-heartedly for many years, mastering numerous techniques and receiving high ranks. I also asked how, why and what if - a lot - in an eager attempt to learn but also with some innate skepticism. Highly choreographed exhibitions where senior-aged instructors were able to overwhelm seemingly endless numbers of young, strong attackers, at the same time, were more than suspect. I enthusiastically volunteered when master martial artists needed someone to demonstrate their devastating techniques on. It's called "Feeling the hands of the master." For me, I wanted to know exactly how these techniques worked and what they felt like. I wanted to know what in martial arts was real and what was myth, hype and good showmanship. Some styles have a very devoted following who do little questioning of their senseis (instructors). Some instructors, with large egos, might interpret a student's questioning of a technique's application and viability as challenging and disrespectful. Other instructors' welcome scrutiny and have much depth to draw from. For the most part, in my travels, I found genuine people doing their best to pass on a tradition and what they found valuable. In my dojo, or to-chang (Korean for school), the aim is to build the students' capabilities, character and confidence.

Some say that martial arts training and self-defense training are different animals and that karate doesn't work when faced with real-life violence. I agree with a lot of that. But there are many different styles of martial arts. Some focus on traditional forms and classical movement. Others emphasize physical combat with varying degrees of contact being allowed in practice. In my training over the years with "master instructors" (a totally subjective title, by the way), I recognized that some of the concepts being taught, although well-intentioned, were lacking in judgment and were potentially dangerous, putting a student at greater risk.

I once asked one of my master instructors, who had been teaching for 30 years, what to do if you were held-up at gunpoint. The answer he gave is shocking to me now but at the time I supposed my instructor knew what he was talking about. He was older and experienced, right? He wouldn't give bad advice, would he? He was wearing a black belt with many stripes on it indicating his high rank. He spoke with such authority. In this scenario, even though he was offering what he thought made sense, he was dead wrong. Without any inquiry into the circumstances of the situation such as the setting, number of assailants, their mental state, their age, where the players were positioned, type and number of potential weapons present, what the demands were, and what other options may be available, he told me that if the gun was in range, even though pointing at you, you should kick it. KICK IT?! Did I hear that right? Because he was a tournament point fighter, he was good at getting points by kicking so, his advice was to kick the gun. Hmmmm.... I guess the kick hits the gun or wrist perfectly and magically disarms the assailant so you can, somehow, move in, subdue him, recover the weapon and restrain him or them, until the police get there. You imagine the police will escort the bad guy/s out and thank you for your public service and incredible bravery while being thoroughly impressed with your martial arts adeptness. But, doesn't kicking the gun actually increase the chances of it going off? Questioning would be seen as challenging and disrespectful.

About six months later a friend of mine was working in a convenience store late one evening when a man wearing a hoodie walked behind the counter, pointed a gun at him and demanded the money in the cash drawer. My friend, who had trained in karate for about a year, kicked at the gun. The gun went off, the bullet hitting him in the shoulder. No big deal, right? We've all seen the movies where the hero simply fights on after putting some gauze on the wound or someone announces that the bullet went clean through. The hero continues barely noticing that he was shot. Not in this case. The bullet that hit my friend in the shoulder, ricocheted off a bone and cut across both lungs, causing massive hemorrhaging. He died before help arrived. His martial arts moves and self-defense strategy got him killed where if he had done nothing, odds are, he would have been talking to the police as they filled out the robbery report. I learned to question everything.

INTRODUCTION

This book was written to help equip you mentally and physically for effective self-defense against intimidation and assault.

One of the most essential needs of the human condition is the need to feel safe. It is number two on Maslow's Hierarchy of Human Needs proceeded only by the physical necessities of life. I believe that every human wants to be able to protect themselves, their family and their stuff; to have some control over their own security, and peace of mind.

The world is a dangerous place. Denial of that truth will leave you vulnerable to those who would do you harm. Over-attention to the fact can cause excessive fear and paranoia which could wreck your life. Your destiny may never be realized.

We do a lot to minimize the dangers in our lives. We lock our doors, fix frayed electrical cords, pick up children's toys off of the stairs, replace bald tires on our cars and wear sunblock. But how much time do we devote to preventing the horrible personal violation of assault and rape which, if experienced, will change your life and the lives of those around you. There are ways to minimize the risk from predators. I hope you agree that it's worth your time to prepare.

I hope that this book will help you not only protect you and yours but also empower you. One corporate owner, whose team attended one of my seminars, put it this way: "This is an empowerment program like no other. Using a smooth and sophisticated martial arts approach, Rick guides people through a process of discovery that frees them from a variety of self-limiting assumptions to see grander visions and new possibilities for personal and professional transformation."* If we can engage possibility thinking with a little effort, we can have greater control over our circumstances, our safety and our well-being. We can take advantage of the resources available in any given situation and use them to our advantage. *(Dr Rod Bartell

Founder of Bartell &Bartell, Ltd, Center for Executive Assessment and Development)

This life is a BYOB event (Be Your Own Bodyguard). That thought is worthy of some serious consideration. Being skillful at personal protection will take some time and training. It will take a serious mind and following some daily disciplines. But it is necessary if you want the best chances of being safe from predators. Never leave something as important as your life and your health to others, e.g., friends, family, spouse, police. Nobody can care for you as well as you. Even if you have a paid private security detail, it is still important to be ready and able to protect yourself and your family.

Mark Twain said:

> "A human being is the product of two factors: heredity and training. Since heredity cannot be altered after the fact, training is the only important variable in human success. There is nothing training cannot do. The essential thing is to get good training instead of bad training."

There are no "Easy Steps to Self Defense" or "Self-Defense in Seconds" as some books are titled. The reality is that serious personal safety takes effort. It takes knowledge, awareness and confronting uncomfortable truths. We have to deal with fear, form safety habits and execute defense protocols. It takes practice but you can take charge of your life without dedicating years to martial arts training. In short, it's about awareness and preparation.

The tactical information in this book came from my decades of experience and research working with the martial arts, law enforcement and military communities. It came from the stories of real-life people who have been in difficult situations and what they learned that can help us today.

This book is for those who are willing to stand strong for their rights and pursuit of happiness. I wish I had known this information in grade school. Life would have been a lot easier. But I'm thankful I know it now. You will be too. After reading, and applying some of the information in this book, you will be better equipped to achieve the victories that await you.

Chapter 1
DEFINITIONS

Martial Arts

In the martial arts we, many times, see traditionalized combat and self-defense widely practiced as sport. Some examples are Judo, Karate (a general term for many styles of martial arts) kick boxing and others.

Point sparring competitions may or may not have any real combat application. Competitors can stack up trophies and still be unprepared for real physical combat against one or more armed or unarmed assailants.

Martial means military. In mythology, Mars was the Roman god of war, one of the patron gods of Rome. He was responsible for everything military. Therefore, the term martial art first referred to the craft of military cunning and war.

This book is not about sport or winning trophies. It's about survival. I use some martial arts techniques and disciplines along with other things to accomplish that end.

Self-Defense

Self-defense is a reasonable countermeasure that involves defending the health and well-being of oneself or others from harm. The use of the "right of self-defense" as a legal justification for the use-of-force in times of danger is available in many jurisdictions in the United States, but the interpretation of that standard can vary widely. Check and know your local laws regarding this use-of-force in regard to self-protection. You don't want to be in a situation where you are charged with excessive force in your response.

Simply put: You have the right to use the least amount of force that any reasonable person would believe necessary to successfully protect themselves from perceived imminent harm.

Brief History of Our Presumed Right to Safety Here in the U.S.

In this country, we are presumed to have a reasonable expectation of safety and the right to pursue happiness. That's not the case everywhere in the world. Take a quick look at some of our founding document's wording regarding to this concept.

"The Virginia Declaration of Rights was written in 1776 primarily by George Mason to proclaim the inherent rights of men. It influenced later documents including our United States Declaration of Independence. Section 1 of the Virginia Declaration provides, "That all men are by nature equally free and independent and have certain inherent rights, of which, when they enter into a state of society, they cannot, by any compact, deprive or divest their posterity; namely, the enjoyment of life and liberty, with the means of acquiring and possessing property, and pursuing and obtaining happiness and **safety**."" Stay with me here.

(Excerpt from Library of Congress) (National Archives - Virginia's Declaration of Rights Section 1.)

The Pennsylvania Constitution or 'Declaration of Rights' authored mainly by Benjamin Franklin and the Massachusetts Declaration of Rights amongst whose authors were John Adams and Samuel Adams specifically refer to pursuing and obtaining happiness and **safety** as a basic human right.

Our own U.S. Declaration of Independence states: "We hold these truths to be self-evident, that all men are created equal, that they are endowed by their Creator with certain unalienable rights, that among these are life, liberty and the pursuit of happiness."

John Lock, whose writings influenced our founding fathers, said, "The state of Nature has a law of Nature to govern it which obliges everyone, and reason, which is that law, teaches all mankind who will but consult it, that being all equal and independent, **no one ought to harm another in life, health, liberty or possessions....**" (Quote: John Lock - Second Treatise of Government Chapter 2, State of Nature.)

Understanding human rights and how to best structure a civil society, setting up laws based, in part, on the Golden Rule does not mean that everyone will obey those laws.

The crime rate for rape, aggravated assault and overall violent crime rose significantly since 1960.

U.S. 1960 Crime Rate Per 100,000 people

Forcible Rape - 9.6

Aggravated Assault - 86.1

Overall Violent Crime - 160.9

2015 Crime Rate Per 100,000 people

Forcible Rape - 28.1

Aggravated Assault - 237.8

Overall Violent Crime - 382.2

That's a 200 - 300% percent increase in all three categories!

At the writing of this book crime is skyrocketing around the country as police departments are being defunded and restricted causing massive personnel shortages. Many criminals who in the past would be charged and jailed are back out on the street because of no bail policies and some prosecutors are not choosing to prosecute some crimes. Hopefully that will change and our system will support safer communities.

The Problem

Society doesn't protect us. Predators don't respect us. Some among us choose the dark side at times and inflict violence and every form of evil upon others. We have wars and books on war, like Sun Tzu's "The Art of War." We have law enforcement and courts to help keep violent offenders off the streets but sadly law enforcement and the courts are inadequate in preventing crime. Police officers, as much as they would love to prevent crime, usually show up after the fact and take reports and sometimes make arrests. Your personal safety is, therefore, your responsibility.

There can be serious consequences to planning or not planning to address potential hostility in your life. The good news is, there are simple behaviors and precautions that you can employ that greatly decrease your chances of being victimized.

Don't:

1. Put your head in the sand and hope for the best.
2. Believe that others will protect you.
3. Keep a big dog with you at all times.
4. Live blissfully assured that bad things don't happen to good people like you.

I was teaching a personal safety course at Christian College, when a student said to me, "I don't have to worry about being assaulted, I'm a good Christian." I thought to myself, didn't they attack and crucify Jesus and many of his followers? How does this student believe that Christians are immune to violence? But she needed to feel safe, as we all do, so she eagerly embraced a myth.

The reality is that violence happens and we need to be our own, full-time, bodyguards. Your safety and that of your loved ones is your responsibility. I was raised, being taught that as the male in a relationship or family, I have a duty to protect. That upbringing was a gift to me and it carries a great responsibility. But it's not only for males. With practice, you can be proficient at being not being a victim— a "hard target" (not an easy target). No previous training or expertise is needed.

The physical defense techniques presented in this book are not necessarily size or strength specific. They are based on physics, leverage, speed, surprise, shock and awe, violence of action, pressure points and affective targeting with commitment. By applying **risk reduction strategies** and increasing your **perceptual range** you will see a potential threat early and be able to lessen the opportunity of being victimized or avoid the situation altogether.

Overwhelming statistics show that just having the willingness to fight back against aggression puts you in a much better position than surrendering and assuming that you have no good options.

One thought here. There are many success stories where people championed their right to live-out-loud and prevailed in difficult situations. You will read many in this book. But sometimes things just go wrong. You do everything right but you can't control every circumstance. My son, who was in the Air Force, and I were discussing the June 28, 2005 mission and firefight in Kabul Afghanistan where Marcus Latrell was the only Navy Seal to come out alive. My son said, "Ya dad, …. that was a bad day for those guys." We were quiet for a few seconds. There are no guarantees. We just have to do our best every day and fight on. Living on, being all you can be and all you "might have been" robs the enemy of a long-term victory. ("It's never too late to be all you might have been," quote from George Eliot - one of my favorites.)

Unfortunately, there are no guarantees.

Chapter 2

YOUR MINDSET MATTERS

"Whether you believe you can do a thing or can't you are right." (Henry Ford)

Mindset is your attitude. It's 90% of the battle. You can have all the right tools for effective self-defense but if you are not willing to use them, they are useless.

I once asked the ladies in my class (an all-female class) about their resolve in fighting back against an assault. One woman spoke up and said she would never be able to fight for herself. She would rather just submit and take her chances. I asked her if she had children. She had three. I asked her what she might be willing to do if she knew that the attacker would move to the kids after her? She looked intently at me. I literally saw a change in her eyes and her breathing. Her posture radiated intense energy. She said, "I would tear them apart. Nothing is going to hurt my kids." There we go, I thought. It's important to remember that we are fighting for more than ourselves. What affects us affects everyone close to us. Remember that you are fighting for your daughter's mother (that's you), your granddaughter's grandmother (that's you). If you're a man, then you're fighting for your child's father (you). Our kids need us fully functional.

The most beneficial self-defense mindset is one that seeks to eliminate our blind spots (areas of vulnerability) and then to not just get angry about others thinking they can take advantage of you, get absolutely indignant about it. How dare they? Do they think you're just going to lie down and surrender? Oh, I don't think so. We are not just going to say no, we are going to say, "Oh hell no! Not today M** F**. You mess with me and it's going to be a bad day for you. I will fight with everything I have.

I'm all in and among other things, I can bite really hard." I know these are uncomfortable and intense ideas but remember we are talking about survival. Nice doesn't cut it when someone is looking at you as lunch. And we are worth fighting for.

I have worked with survivors of rape and assault. Some seek help to get back to themselves, some., believe it or not, use their trauma to become better and stronger than they have ever been and now help teach and empower others. Lady D, as I will refer to her, a rape survivor, came to me after having taken 2 other self-defense courses. After my program she said that she regained her confidence and "Got her life back." She went on to help others who had experienced rape trauma. A good book titled "Antifragile" describes a mindset of using every ambiguity, error and trial to, not just get by, but to get stronger.

Author Taleb states, "Antifragility is beyond resilience or robustness. The resilient resist shocks and stays the same; the antifragile get better."

(Antifragile: Things That Gain from Disorder by Nassim Nicholas Taleb, Copyright © 2012 by Nassim Nicholas Taleb. Random House Publishing ISBN 978-1-4000-6782-4)

Mushin is Japanese for "mind of no mind." It means you get to decide what matters to you and what doesn't. You can pay attention to a thing or not. What you decide to dwell on matters. If assaulted, most physical scars fade away in time but the emotional scars, those traumas, thoughts and memories that we allow to occupy too much real estate in our minds, can plague us far too long. They can quiet our voices. It is the goal of this training to help you live out loud, gather your strength and sail your ship. (

> "I am not afraid of the storms for I am learning how to sail my ship." Louisa May Alcott

The Hard Target Mindset

People who are hard targets, a military term meaning hard to kill, capture or fool, take the time to prepare for the fight. They gear up with knowledge, body armor, weapons, night vision, GPS, armored vehicles, intel, teams and strategy. But none of that would be enough to accomplish the mission and come home alive if they didn't have the survival mindset.

We must be prepared in mind and body. We have to be physically able and mentally willing to unleash hell if necessary. We need to be vigilant, know the environment, know the objective, navigate the landscape and execute the plan. An 8th-degree black belt friend of mine, Dwight, describes unleashing your power as "letting the dragon out." It comes with a vocal shout seasoned with a growl as you throw the switch or move mentally and physically to a place where you will do whatever it takes. It's the part of us that we keep quiet unless we enter the jungle (a place known to be dangerous) and decide to go to war. Sadly, many people, including me at an earlier age, aren't prepared for the savagery and evil that a small percentage of the population is capable of....or maybe many of us in the right wrong circumstances. We think that everyone thinks like us and that by being kind and trying to reason with an assailant, we can talk them out of their intentions. I wouldn't count on it.

My job is not to understand the attacker's mind, except, as it would help me to avoid danger, if I can, or prevail against it if I can't. We have options, in most situations when potential violence enters our lives. We can attempt to defuse. We can trick with psychological ploys to gain an advantage. Example: One woman told a guy who was attempting to rape her that it was a bad time of the month for her and asked him to come back in a week. He actually agreed and when he returned a week later, he was met by her and the police. We can also use physical force and adaptive weapons (things that are easily accessible that we can use as a weapon) which might include: a pen, keys, a chair. Or we can train and use actual weapons: gun, knife, club, chemical agents (pepper spray) and stun guns. We can also employ electronics, phones, and tracking apps to aid us. Tracking apps monitor our movements and send an alert to a designated party if you deviate from the route or are late in arriving at your destination.

Cooper's Color Code System

Col. Jeff Cooper (U.S. Marines) developed a color code system to help warriors gauge their mindset for combat scenarios. It's useful in self-defense. In relaxed alert (yellow) situational awareness helps to detect a potential threat and consider options that you are willing to take. In orange, we set mental triggers that, if tripped, we act. In red, the triggers have been tripped and we act. (This information is used with permission from Ken Campbell, Chief Executive Officer, Gunsight Academy, Inc. Founded by Col. Jeff Cooper)

Col. Jeff Cooper's Color Code System

White	Unprepared and unready to take action.
Yellow	Prepared, alert & relaxed. Good situational awareness.
Orange	Alert to probable danger. Ready to take action.
Red	Action Mode. Focused on the emergency at hand.
Black	Panic. Breakdown of physical & mental performance.

My wife, then girlfriend, said she was heading out with a friend to a bar in downtown Grand Rapids. I cautioned her to be careful as it was getting late. They were two nice looking ladies out alone. She assured me that everything would be fine. At about 11:00 pm she called me very upset. She explained that a large man pushed his way into her booth, uninvited, and grabbed her phone. She stood up to him and got her phone back, then, when he stepped away for a moment, she quickly called me saying she needed my help. I was headed home from a gathering. I spun my car around and got there about 12 minutes later, parking right in front of the bar doors. I walked in, asked one of the security guards to follow me, then walked around looking for the ladies. When I found them, they said the guy had gone into another room in the back of the bar.

9

I had to get home to my son so I was unable to stay and resolve the situation further. I introduced my girlfriend to the security guard, informed him of the problem and asked if he would personally monitor the situation if they decided to stick around. He said sure. Turns out a short time later, the guy picked a fight with someone else in the backroom and was escorted out. The ladies finished the evening now more aware of how quickly things can change. My wife started in Cooper's white zone (never expecting any trouble, assuming her safety) and jumped right to red (action mode). One important part of this story is my wife's mindset after being confronted. She wasn't going to be intimidated. She acted by demanding and then taking her phone back. She stood up for herself and then called for backup. There's no doubt in my mind that if the guy had gotten more aggressive with her, he would have had a fight on his hands. She is no pushover. Part of good defensive tactics is to utilize what the environment offers. There were big, strong guys employed to protect the patrons. So, we used that option and all was well.

Cooper takes issue with how his color system has been interpreted. He comments that "There is a problem in that some students insist upon confusing the appropriate color with the amount of danger evident in the situation. As I have long taught, you are not in any color state because of the specific amount of danger you may be in, but rather in a mental state which enables you to take a difficult psychological step. Now, however, the government has gone into this and is handing out color codes nationwide based upon the apparent nature of a peril. We cannot say that the government's ideas about colors are wrong, but that they are different from what we have long taught here at Gunsite (firearms training academy). The problem is this: your combat mindset is not dictated by the amount of danger to which you are exposed at the time. Your combat mindset is properly dictated by the state of mind you think appropriate to the situation. It depends upon the willingness you have to jump a psychological barrier against taking irrevocable action."

We are always in one of Cooper's colors, mental states.

White

You are switched off, unaware and vulnerable due, possibly, to:

- You are uninformed as to life's dangers
- Distractions
- Being fatigued or sleep-deprived
- Being impaired by drugs and alcohol
- You're lazy minded and hoping for the best

Your reaction might be, "Oh my God, how is this happening to me?"

Yellow

You are educated and wary. You are alert, not paranoid. Your experience has taught you that people getting too close and in certain emotional states can escalate and be dangerous. You've taken a self-defense course and obtained a concealed pistol license so you are prepared to take action should you detect the need. Cooper's mindset in yellow is "I may have to shoot today."

Ideally, we want to be in level yellow all the time. We want to be relaxed and alert, comfortable that I'm prepared to handle situations that might arise. I don't want to be oblivious and vulnerable nor do I want to be stressed, anxious and on alert all the time. We can shoot for competent and confident.

Orange

Something has caught your attention. There is a specific threat. Cooper's mindset moves to "I may have to shoot *that* person today." You are ready to take action. You may evade, hide, arm yourself or employ any strategy that makes sense to you.

Red

This is action mode. The fight is on. Someone has demonstrated a direct threat to you. You have the legal right to self-defense and are going to use it. Cooper says, "You are in lethal mode and *will* shoot if circumstances warrant it."

The goal is always to get clear of danger using the least amount of force necessary. Recognizing attack patterns, and pre-fight rituals will help avoid level red.

Chapter 3
MYTHS AND MISCONCEPTIONS

Here are some common misconceptions that could influence your self-defense strategies.

1. I might get hurt worse if I resist.
    Many studies including from The National Institute of Mental Health found that there is no more chance of getting injured by fighting back and that you are twice as likely to escape, knowing no self-defense, just by resisting.

2. Someone will help me if I scream.
    This story, and now famous study, may change your mind. Kitty Genovese, March 13th, 1964, New York City - neighbors and bystanders witnessed her being stabbed to death on a sidewalk in a busy neighborhood. No one intervened or called the police. The assailant was later captured. Chief of Detectives Albert A. Seedman asked the killer how he dared to attack a woman in front of so many witnesses, according an article by Seedman & Peter Hellman, the psychopath calmly replied, "I knew they wouldn't do anything. People never do." This prompted research into the bystander effect and "diffusion of responsibility concept" — a tendency for people not to get involved when others are present.

    —Article: Seedman & Peter Hellman, 1974. The Kitty Genovese story. Used by permission from Peter Hellman

Husbands, boyfriends, family and bystanders cannot be depended on. Police get there afterward. Susan B Anthony said, "I declare to you that woman must not depend upon the protection of man but must be taught to protect herself, and there I take my stand." (Quote taken from literature written in the late 1800s during the women's suffrage movement.)

My friend Samantha told me that she was walking to her car when a youth came up to her and grabbed her purse. Sam held on to the strap. He hit her in the face knocking her to the ground. I said, Sam, what were you thinking. Why didn't you let go? It's only stuff. She said, "It's my purse." He pulled harder. She held on. He kicked her in the head. She let go. The youth <u>walked</u> off with the purse. No one helped even though there were bystanders less than 20 feet away. Sam was surprised that no one intervened on her behalf. She sustained bruises. The sad truth is you can't count on people to get involved. And it's not their fault.

3. I'll become a catalyst for his anger if I resist.
   They are already angry. Remember that fighting, or resistance, can take many forms. Be strategic. Look for an opening. People who commit assault and rape fit into different psychological profiles, some more dangerous than others. There is no one size fits all defense. Types of rapists:

   - Power /Assertive
   - Anger / Retaliation
   - Aggressive Aim
   - Sadistic

4. I can talk my way out of it.
   A rapist, on average, commits seven rapes before being caught. They are experienced and don't care about your rights or feelings. You are an object to them. And the recidivism rate for a prisoner who is released from prison, for the crimes of rape and murder, is 83%. That's five out of six prisoners that get arrested again within nine years of being released. You may be dealing with a career criminal. But talking and tricking are options that have worked in some cases.

5. I can't defend against a big guy.
    In a fight between a 100-lb. dog vs. an 8-lb. cat, if you throw water on the cat (making him mad), my money is on the cat. It's not just size and strength that wins but surprise, violence of action, explosion and determination. The goal, remember, is just to create enough space and time to get clear of danger.

6. It's not feminine to be aggressive.
    Is this fair? Does this one concern anyone? It's ok to act out of character when so much is at stake. Prepare early. Go to war if necessary and put femininity aside.

7. Rape is only a sex crime.
    Rape is a savage assault that will change your life forever. It is the sexual expression of anger, hostility, control, dominance and abuse.

8. I'll just kick him "you know where" (the groin).
    Ok, good thought, and it might work but consider this too:

    •   It's a small target
    •   It puts you off balance because the target is high off the ground
    •   Kicks to the groin are difficult and men expect it

9. I have a rape whistle and pepper spray.
    They have to be quickly accessible. Don't neglect developing other options also.

10. I could never hurt anyone.
    Yes, you can. This brings us back to the question of what you are willing to do. Remember you are not just fighting for you. Most, if not all, of the women I have worked with who suffered an assault, said that if it ever happened again, they would fight with everything they had. Remember that fighting takes many forms. It's not just physical.

    Studies show women who resisted an attacker using flee or try to flee, talk loudly, scream, use physical force and environmental intervention (using your environment to your advantage) were significantly more likely than non-resisters to avoid rape.

(read: The Effect of Victim Resistance on Rape Completion: A Meta-Analysis by Jennifer S Wong, Samantha Balemba, August 12, 2016, Research Article)

Model Mugging Statistics

11. I'm uncomfortable with confrontation.

Most people are. Can we face our discomfort and fears and be effective? Yes. One of my students, a 24-year-old woman, told me that she was a singer. She performs in local productions here in town. She seemed quite confident. I asked her if she could sing for the class, right now, without accompaniment; not thinking she would say yes. To my surprise, she walked to the front of the room announced what song she would be singing and then sang a beautiful song for us. I asked her how she got over the fear of performing. "It's not that I'm not afraid," she said, "I just do it afraid." Fantastic. That's forward aggressive.

12. I think I would freak out.

When we are threatened, our autonomic nervous system (ANS) flies into action. A chemical cocktail of epinephrine (adrenaline), norepinephrine, cortisone, opioid peptides (pain blockers) endorphins and many other hormones dump into our system. Our body is preparing for what's next. With training and by thinking through possible threats, we can move through stress and perform. Military personnel do it, we can too. I will cover our ANS further in another chapter.

13. If I carry a gun, it might be taken and used against me.

A gun brings lethal force to the equation. It's a great idea to carry if you develop proficiency. Know the law and get proper training. Be aware that police are only17% to 52% successful in hitting their target when shooting under stress. You have to be able to access your gun, chamber a round (in automatic handguns), if you don't have one in the chamber already, then be able to hit your target under stressful conditions. All very possible with training.

Chapter 4
THE VICTORY MODEL

Years ago, I came up with what I call the Victory Model. Victory is an acronym for some of the major areas of personal protection from assault. The model covers the following:

Visuals - What we see. What others see.
Intonation - What our voice tone and volume say.
Content - Word choice matters.
Territory - The spaces we choose to protect; boundaries.
Orientation - Positioning of our mind and body to be effective.
Risk analysis - Accurate assessment of a real or perceived threat.
Your call - Your choices and their consequences are yours alone.

To understand how to minimize our vulnerability to assault and reduce the risk of even being targeted, we have to be aware of the signals we send to others and those others are sending to us.

According to Dr. Albert Mehrabian, author of "Silent Messages" (1981), When it comes to communicating our emotions, 55% of our communication is body language and is perceived visually (**V**ictory). Thirty-eight percent is our voice's intonation (V**i**ctory) comprised of tone, tonality and volume. It's perceived audibly. Only seven percent of what we communicate consists of the literal words we use.

Silent messages: Implicit communication of emotions and attitudes by Albert Mehrabian, Copywrite © 1971 by Albert Mehrabian).

Publisher - Belmont, CA, Wadsworth Publishing Company (currently being distributed by Albert Mehrabian)

These three factors, body language, our tone and our words have to be congruent for the communication to be perceived as credible. If someone is stomping their feet, hands clenched and yelling I'm not angry, you might think, "Ya right." The message is not believable. A smile, open hands and a calm voice saying, "I care about you" is more believable. When the voice and body messages don't match, believe the body because words lie easier!

Whatever the exact percentages of our communication are from interaction to interaction, the point is to learn what makes communication effective, and then use it.

Visuals V

What you communicate influences your perceived strength or vulnerability. Because our visual presence is such a major factor in communication, it's important to understand and manage our body language so we don't inadvertently advertise vulnerability and attract the wrong attention. Skill in reading others and picking up on cues of what someone may be contemplating is also critically important.

Detecting aggression early gives us a better chance for an effective defense. The earlier the better.

Ritualized Combat

Police trainer, Roland Ouelette of Canada, termed the phrase Ritualized Combat to describe body language that the human body, in most cases, will go through prior to initiating an assault on another person. If we recognize some of these, finding ourselves in a threatening situation, we can get our hands up, create distance, and try to deescalate the aggression. If we believe assault is imminent, based on his scientific research, we can, in many courts, legally, preemptively strike first. Here is Roland's list of pre-fight characteristics.

Assault Not Imminent but Possible

- Head, neck and shoulders go back (trying to look bigger)
- Face is red—twitching and jerking
- Lips pushed forward baring teeth (same as dogs before an attack)
- Breathing is fast and shallow
- Beads of sweat appear about the face and neck
- Thousand-mile stare
- Exaggerated movements
- Finger-pointing—head pecking motion
- Totally ignores you
- Give you excessive attention—direct eye contact
- Goes from uncooperative to cooperative
- Acts stoned or drunk
- Directs anger towards other objects

Assault Imminent

- Face goes from red to white
- Lips tighten over teeth
- Breathing is fast and deep
- Change of stance—body blades, shoulder drops
- Hands close into a fist—white knuckles
- Bobbing up and down or rocking back and forth on feet
- Target glance—looking at what to strike
- Putting head and chin down to protect airway
- Eyebrows brought forward in a frown
- Stops all movement
- Dropping center or lowering body
- Sheds clothing
- One syllable replies—reptilian brain (fight or flight)

In this group, with assault being perceived as imminent, according to Roland, you will have approximately 1 to 1.5 seconds to act before your attacker does. He says, "Striking first is critical." In my opinion, striking first is only one, possibly good, option.

Another strategy that may be helpful, that I have used, is to bring to the attention of the aggressor what you are seeing, the behavior that they are exhibiting. The reasons are:

1. The aggressor may not be aware of what they are doing.
2. Some attackers will only attack when they believe that they have the element of surprise. By sharing with them what you see, you take this tactic away from them.

Roland also states that there are times when you should not let the person know what you are seeing so you can use the element of surprise to your advantage!

(Ritualized Combat information and comments by Roland Ouellette and Darren Laur; USAdojo.com)

I got to see some of Roland's preflight characteristics first hand. I was involved in a minor confrontation in a post office where a man tried to nudge in front of me to be waited on. When I stepped back in front and handed my envelope over the counter, he got furious and threatened to "get me" when we went outside. The clerk was very nervous. When I stepped out of the building, he came toward me. He took off his jacket, threw it on the ground (sheds clothing), and tried to close the distance between us while clenching his fists and swearing at me. Not too hard to read his intentions with that body language, right? He also verbally told me what he was going to do. I put my open hands up, bladed my stance and calmly said this wasn't a good idea. He was still furious but didn't launch any strikes. I told him that if he started, it was going to get ugly. He hesitated a few seconds. He may have thought, "Who's this smaller guy being so calm and confident?" Then without another word, he turned, walked to his car and left. Truth is I *was* confident. I was poised but also ready. I knew exactly what I was going to do if he took another half step towards me. For whatever reason, he left.

Another time I watched two teenage boys in a parking lot surrounded by teenage and adult bystanders. Girls were yelling "Fight! Fight!" The two boys were faced off arguing when one did the classic move—get close, drop one hand to the side with a half turn away and then quickly turn back punching the other boy in the face. The kid that got hit just stood there stunned, and probably embarrassed. A few seconds went by and then people stepped in. If they hadn't stepped in the kid that got hit, who I perceived as totally innocent, probably would have gotten clocked again. Adult onlookers, which included one of the kids' dad, didn't expect the rapid acceleration in violence. Neither did his son. It happened after a friendly teenage baseball tournament. But when emotions are high and someone moves close, close enough to hit you, you have to get your hands up, create some distance and be ready, or engage. You can always try walking away too.

I have a friend, whom I will call Bob, of decent size and strength, who's an executive at a major corporation in. He's a guy who's not afraid to fight. He and his brother-in-law, Dale, were in a restaurant, sitting at the bar. Dale was talking to a stranger who was getting riled up and looking intense. He was giving the 1000-mile stare, his lips tightened and he leaned closer. Bob sensed that Dale was about to get clobbered so he reached in front and punched the guy in the face knocking him off the bar-stool. Nothing else happened. The guy got up and left. It was fortunate that Bob had the awareness to see the imminent threat and preemptively strike first. If this went to court, Bob would have had to articulate his perception of the threat and his reasonable response to protect Dale. You have heard the "who threw the first punch?" question as criteria for determining who was the aggressor in a fight but that is not the only consideration in every case. Sometimes hitting first can be your best option.

The first three letters of the **Victory Model**—VIC (Visual, Intonation and Content) cover communication.

Visual—Non-verbal communication

Intonation—Voice quality. Used well, it can increase the effectiveness of your message.

Content—Words can be powerful. The following are a few examples of what words can do:

1. Defuse and deescalate
2. Decrease interaction time by ending a conversation
3. Educate / instigate

4. Manipulate / intimidate / dominate
5. Command / reprimand
6. Celebrate / validate
7. Impress / express
8. Convince / sway / pray
9. Motivate / infuriate
10. Reveal your intellect or lack of

In addition:

- "The well-wrought word is more powerful than a standing army." (Napoleon)
- "He mobilized the English language and sent it into battle." (Edward R. Murrow's War Speech on Churchill 1940)
- "A word spoken in due season; how good it is."
  (Prov. 15:23 NKJV Bible - Scripture taken from the New King James Version®. Copyright © 1982 by Thomas Nelson. Used by permission. All rights reserved.)
- "A soft answer turns away wrath but a harsh word stirs up anger." (Prov. 15:1 23 NKJV Bible - Scripture taken from the New King James Version®. Copyright © 1982 by Thomas Nelson. Used by permission. All rights reserved.)

Language skill, both verbal and non-verbal is about communication and the power to influence.

To be understood by others, we need to be clear about what it is that we intend to communicate and how best to do that. Amy Cuddy did a popular Ted Talk called "Your Body Language May Shape Who You Are." She states, "We know our non-verbals govern how other people think and feel about us.", and she poses the question, "Do our non-verbals govern how we feel about ourselves?" And there is some evidence that it may. But I am not as interested in how to reprogram our psychology and physiology through poses as I am in knowing how to use power postures to signal a would-be assailant of my willingness to be a very bad victim. The first impression that I want to give is one of strength, confidence and adroitness. Power dynamics, the non-verbal expressions of power and dominance, in the animal kingdom is about expanding and making yourself big. You see it in a lion's mane, a puffer-fish puffing up, a swan charging with wings spread wide, and a cobra spreading out its threatening hood and standing as high as 6 feet tall. People do the same thing. Some men and women take up more space and get bigger when they want to establish authority and power. We give off a larger aura. Observe when people shake hands for the first time. It may be subtle but we don't usually shrink. We let others know that we are alpha. We stand tall, shoulders back, chest out, lean in a little, feet apart and make eye contact. When sitting, we often have our legs apart, hands clasped behind the head with elbows while women, in the past, have been taught that it's more proper and feminine to sit with legs or ankles crossed, arms in and hands on the knees or lap, taking up little space. For our self-defense purposes, we are going to use power postures and gestures to communicate strength, a hard target.

Postures showing weakness and insecurity, taking up little space.

 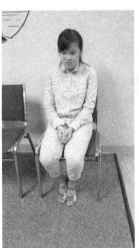 

Confident postures

Cobra

 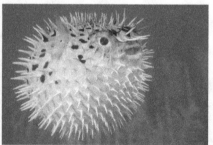

Puffer-fish before and after

Power Poses

Like the puffer-fish, we can puff up too.

You can assume a pose that shows weakness, strength or something in between. With slumped shoulders, looking down, hands in close, feet together, you portray the least confident demeanor possible. Or, we can do a superhero pose. We all know what that looks like. It's what we've seen in movies, cartoons and comic books our whole lives. We have been programmed to recognize these poses as powerful. Why? Because the characters who exhibit these postures perform extraordinary deeds with great courage.

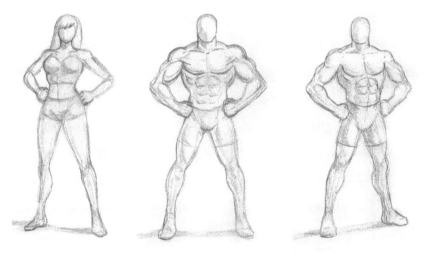

Superhero Poses

Looks do matter but, an important point here; you don't have to be powerful to look powerful. You can fake it. It looks the same and can be effective. Remember the goal is not to be targeted as easy prey based on the way we look. We either want to be unnoticed, which some call the gray man (someone who blends in), or be noticed as assured and powerful, i.e., a hard target.

I once was coming down a flight of stairs at my college apartment complex to see a guy, much larger than me, playing with his girlfriend in the hallway. Or so I thought. He was pushing her against a wall and slapping at her as she was trying to fight him off. Thinking it was just play, I decided to join in, as I knew the girl. Totally acting now; I leaped from the 3rd step into the hallway aggressively, like superman dropping in. They both stopped and looked at me as I made two fists and spread out my arms, feet wide apart (my best superhero pose) and said loudly, "Unhand that woman!" He immediately turned, thought for a second, and walked away. My laser stare was still burning through his head. She jumped into my arms shaking and thanking me. She was shaken, terrified. She was being assaulted. She said he was getting very aggressive and hurting her. That was real!? I thought to myself. That guy was twice my size. I could have been killed. Actually, had I known she was being hurt, my response may have been much more aggressive. I didn't let on that I was acting. I was happy that I came along when I did and so was she. I learned a valuable lesson. Perception. Belief matters.

I teach four power postures.

1. Superman / Superwoman - feet apart, hands on hips
2. Principal (high school) / Parents - arms folded in front, feet apart
3. MP (military police) - hands clasped behind your back, stand tall
4. Forward aggressive - one foot slightly forward, weight on front foot, finger pointing at face height

Who stands like this? People in charge, people who hold the line, people who don't take crap. You can too. Try it right now. See how your attitude changes with your posture. Add a little snarl. (optional)

Walking

The way we walk says a lot about us. Walking, running or dancing is a form of expression and therefore part of our visual communication. Again, we want to be aware of what signals we may be sending. A confident walk is less likely to be seen as prey-worthy by a predator so you are less likely to be targeted for assault. A confident walk is natural but purposeful. It consists of a good pace that isn't too slow, a long gait but not overstraining. Taking small steps looks like you are scurrying or creeping. Bilateral arm swinging (each arm swings with the motion of the opposing leg) gives you stability and balance. Keep your head up and shoulders back. Look people in the eyes and smile.

Let them be the first to look away. Don't slip into self-doubt and insecurity. Building a confident demeanor takes practice, especially if you're shy or a little introverted. You can practice daily with people on the street that you will never see again. Look up, say "Hi" and nod your head. See what happens. Sadly, many people today are distracted with their handheld devices, oblivious to what is going on right in front of them. We have to be careful not to cripple our awareness and defenses by looking down at our phones.

Inhibitors to peak performance

We are very good at crippling ourselves emotionally. We willingly participate in negative self-talk, question our own competency, credibility and even our self-worth. My friend Zig Ziglar calls it stinkin thinkin. By undermining our self-confidence, we erode our effectiveness and sometimes, even the courage to try. Confidence is essential for a committed self-defense.

Walt Disney said

> "The secret of making dreams come true can be summarized in four Cs. They are curiosity, confidence, courage and consistency; and the greatest of these is confidence."

> "Self-confidence is the first requisite to great undertakings." (Samuel Johnson)

> "As is our confidence, so is our capacity." (William Hazlitt)

If you take martial arts or a self-defense course, you will see just how powerful you are in many ways. With training, you will gain confidence. After just a few weeks of instruction and hitting targets, my 6-year-old students exhibit amazing competence. I wouldn't want to get hit by any of them without holding a foam shield in front of me. We need to let go of assumed self-imposed limitations. Allow yourself to see new horizons and grander visions. I have seen many hundreds of children and adults come into the dojo with low self-esteem, very shy and easily intimidated. They all leave supercharged, having realized more of their inner power. It starts with attitude and the willingness to be open-minded. Determination, the strength of will, combined with technique is formidable. You can do about anything you decide to do. "It's never too late to be all you might have been." (George Eliot)

Intonation I

Intonation is what you sound like; your voice. It's the tone and volume of your utterance. It gives away your emotional state of mind. High tones can communicate panic or emergency while lower, deliberate tones can be humorless and serious. Volume is attention-getting and can accelerate tension, short-circuiting good communication. It can trigger defensiveness and a fight or flight reaction. A confident, reasonable tone is calm, direct and even or measured. With some practice, we can be more deliberate with tone in conversation instead of the reactionary tones that we may default to in some circumstances.

<u>Going Loud</u>

Picture yourself talking very quietly to a friend and then, without warning, you lean in and yell your next words at full volume. I have done this with students in my classes. The reaction is always the same. Everyone gets startled and freezes for a couple seconds. Adrenaline spikes and heart rates skyrocket, then they recover saying it scared them. It's part of our sympathetic nervous system response; part of our survival mechanism. We all can be startled. Knowing this allows us to use it to our advantage, to stun and gain a second or two of time to escape or get clear of danger.

Going loud should be part of our arsenal. This is the theory behind a flash- bang grenade, sometimes called a stun grenade; a little canister that is shot or thrown through an opening before law enforcement enters. It produces a stunningly loud bang of about 170 decibels (a jet engine produces 140 decibels) and a burst of light about 7 million candela (a common candle flame emits about one candela) which overloads the retina causing temporary visual impairment. They're designed to cause non-lethal, temporary disorientation to aid in criminal apprehension. A human being can yell at about 110 to 120 decibels. That enough to startle or stun. Think about if someone grabbed you in a front bear hug, facing you, and as they squeeze or pick you up, you lean in and scream into their ear as loud as you can. People reflexively pull away and reach to cover their ears from loud noises. The technique can cause extreme pain and hearing loss. It's our voice weapon. More on that in a later chapter.

Content C

Content of our communication refers to the actual words we use.

We all know people who wax poetic, use flowery prose and way more words than necessary, droning on and on, their monolog wandering all over the place but saying relatively nothing of interest nor pertaining to any discernible point. That last sentence was an example of just that. These people are not skilled or eloquent speakers, to say the least. I have always appreciated succinctness. In strong self-defense communication, brevity works best.

- "Brevity is the soul of wit." Shakespeare
- "He who has knowledge spares his words..." Prov. 17:27 NKJV Bible Scripture taken from the New King James Version®. Copyright © 1982 by Thomas Nelson. Used by permission. All rights reserved.
- "Be bright, be brief, and be gone." Decker Communications & Sales Co.

Historical examples of short-and-sweet speech.

- "I have a dream..." Martin Luther King Jr.
- "With me." Bruce Lee
- "I'll be back." Terminator
- "Damn the torpedoes." Union Admiral David Farragut
- "I shall return." General Douglas MacArthur
- "That's one small step for man..." Neil Armstrong
- "Follow me..." **Jesus (Matt. 4:19 NKJV** Scripture taken from the New King James Version®. Copyright © 1982 by Thomas Nelson. Used by permission. All rights reserved.

Giving Orders

It's sometimes necessary to give orders to accomplish an objective.

Command language is no-nonsense, short sentences that direct others. Like in dog training, we don't negotiate, we don't have a conversation, we command: sit, fetch, leave it, etc. Here are some examples of command language for people:

- Stop!
- Step back. Step back 5 feet (former prisoners may instinctively respond to this due to hearing it in detention facilities)
- Get back...... GET THE F BACK!
- I don't think so (said defiantly)
- I'm not comfortable with that. You need to stop it.
- Ok, I'm done, that's enough.
- No
- Not today
- No thank you
- F-you (meaning NO!)

You can word-craft and become skillful with your language and have greater influence. Two resources are: "Difficult Conversations" by Douglas Stone, and "How They Said It" by Rosalie Maggio.

Territory T

Our territory is defined as the space that we decide to claim and are willing to defend. We set and maintain boundaries by establishing a perimeter that we want respected and intend to enforce. Some call this their comfort zones. We all have a built-in yard-stick that defines our personal space. Those whom we are close to are welcome in this space. If others invade it, it causes distress. At this point, we are either prepared to address the situation or we need to learn how to address the situation. Animals mark and protect their territories. They have circles of perceived safety and zones of threat. If you approach the outer boundary of that space, they will flee. If you charge through it or cross it unnoticed and get too close, they will instinctively attack or employ their defense mechanism. At this point, the animal has lost the opportunity to flee as the cost of fleeing now outweighs the benefit. The safe flight initiation distance (FID), is where the benefit of fleeing still outweighs the risk.

The term *proxemics* was coined by Edward T. Hall, a noted anthropologist. It describes our comfort zones related to people's proxemics to us (distance from us). We are acutely aware of people within 2 to 6 feet of us and are generally uncomfortable because we instinctively know that we have little reaction time if they become a threat. Distance equals time. Time equals options. One option is to turn and run which is contingent upon our believing we have safe flight initiation distance, FID

Hall describes four zones of space that we in America seem to adhere to in many circumstances. Intimate space - 0 to 18", private space - 18" to 4 feet, social space - 4 to 12 feet and public space is 12 feet and beyond. This is measured by a sensory shift that we experience as we cross over to the next zone. Anyone inside of our intimate space, or what I call "perfume distance," should be by permission only. We need to be aware of our personal comfort zones and be ready to defend them IF we expect to maintain them. Be aware that different cultures have different interpretations of personal space. In Africa, I was greeted with a kiss on both cheeks from a total stranger, according to their culture, which is also reflected in many parts of Europe. That would be uncomfortable in the U.S. but recoiling or showing discomfort would be insulting.

Our territory can be anything from the armrests that we claim in a theatre or on an airplane to the house and yard we protect with fences and walls or the gated neighborhood we choose to live in. The last line of defense that we have direct control over is our body and mind and my disposition regarding me is three words: "Can't touch this." You may, by chance, touch me physically but that which I decide to hold in my mind is mine alone. William James, considered the father of American philosophy, said:

"The greatest discovery of my lifetime is that you can change the quality of your life by changing the quality of your thoughts."

Marcus Aurelius said:

"The happiness of your life depends on the quality of your thoughts, therefore, guard accordingly and take care that you entertain no notions unsuitable to virtue and reasonable nature."

The things we think about matter.

Some language may be offensive to us. We have standards as to how we allow others to treat us and talk to us. In the book "The Gentle Art of Self-Defense" by Suzette Elgin, she says that there are many examples of how to recognize and break the patterns of what we refer to as verbal abuse. People use phrases that imply you are inadequate or stupid compared to others. These sentences often start with "Even you should ..." or "Don't you even...." For example: "Even you should be able to understand." Or, "Even you should be able to do this." Or, "Don't you even care about that?" These are condescending satire modes used by a verbal mugger to do verbal violence to you. Elgin says that some of the best verbal bullies are only 6-years-old. Which reminds me: I was swimming in a lake with my 5 and 6-year-old niece and nephew last summer at a 4th of July party. They complained about not having goggles that worked. I, being courteous, asked my niece if she wanted to borrow my goggles. Her reply was, "Eeew, I don't want old man goggles on my face." What could I say? I just sank slowly underwater and swam away like a dejected hippopotamus. But when it's a person who should know better, you can learn to verbally turn your opponent's energy against them as in Judo. We can practice and get better at confronting intimidation. We don't have to tolerate disrespect and intimidation. Someone tries to bully you? This is going to be a bad day for them because you're a black belt in verbal Judo. A couple of responses to this type of satire is: "Hold it right there. Did you say, 'Even me?' What exactly are you implying?" Or "I'm sorry to stop you but I find your statement and tone condescending."

Safe practices require us to be aware of, claim and protect these lines of demarcation, our boundaries and prepare to maintain them verbally and non-verbally.

The Gentle Art of Verbal Self-Defense by Suzette Haden Elgin. Copywrite © by Suzette Haden Elgin. Publisher - Prentice-Hall, Dorset House Publishing Co Inc.

The Clock

People ask, "How do you keep people from coming up behind you?" To know who is at your 6 (directly behind you) you have to keep your head on a swivel, turning your head 90 degrees in both directions, and use your peripheral vision. It is not hard but we have to get in the habit of checking. We must be aware, increase our perceptual range and be conscious of our natural blind spot to the rear.

Whether you are walking with a friend, driving a car or flying at Mack 2 in an F22 Raptor, you can use the "clock" face for directional reference. Whatever direction you are traveling or facing at the time is considered 12 o'clock; three o'clock is on your right side, six o'clock is directly behind you, nine o'clock is to your left. "Check your 6" is a common term used in law enforcement, the military and other places, meaning, look behind you. You're walking with a friend. There's a suspicious person on your left. You say, "Creeper at 10 o'clock 20 yards out." Without pointing or needless chit chat, you are both on the same page within seconds.

My friend, Tim, a police officer, was working a homicide case where a college student was running on the outdoor track, on campus, late one afternoon listening to music through her earbuds. A man in his late twenties ran up behind her, unnoticed, and hit her in the head with a pipe knocking her unconscious. He then dragged her under the bleachers where he strangled her to death, then, molested and raped her. Other details are not necessary here. The guy was caught and is still in prison. The first thing I tell students is to reduce or eliminate distractions. It's all about awareness, awareness, awareness. Being your own bodyguard is serious. Muted senses cripple alertness, your body's natural ability to warn you of danger. Protecting our territory takes a capable sentry at the gate. You.

Orientation O

Orientation is how we position ourselves mentally and physically to effectively confront a challenge or threat. If we perceive a threat, we want to be ready to quickly move to neutralize it. If we can't eliminate the threat, we want to manage it as well as possible.

Examples:

1. You see three strangers noticing you from a distance. They talk to each other briefly and then change direction and come toward you. You sense there's something wrong. You feel vulnerable so you take action and jump into a cab or run and catch up to others or duck into a crowded coffee shop. Maybe you reach into your purse for your gun. Maybe?

2. Someone bumps your car from behind with theirs. You're cautious realizing that it could be a set-up and you don't like the area you're in. You decide to stay in the car (orientation) and exchange information through the window. If you still feel uncomfortable, you call 911 and give them your location, situation and identification so they know you will not leave the scene before they get there. Or you decide to signal the offender to follow you to another safer location. You have taken action orienting you and your vehicle to manage and mitigate the threat.

Mental orientation is simply setting your mind for the outcome that you desire and what you might have to do to bring that about. There are no guarantees, except that nothing ever goes as planned, but a hard target mindset and pre-thinking situations increase our chances of success.

In an attempted rape situation, you may decide that fighting back means cooperating with the demands of the assailant until you see the opportunity to take action. There was a college student who was in her dorm room sleeping in the top bunk of a bunkbed. She awoke to a guy climbing over her. She was, of course, startled and frightened. Coincidentally, that summer before returning to school, she had taken a self-defense course while on a cruise ship, where she learned an eye gouge maneuver. This is where you cup the back of the attacker's head and drive a thumb into an eye socket. Not a comfortable thought, I know. She waited until he tried to pull the covers down and then hit him with that exact move. He recoiled backward. She held the back of his head and continued. They both fell from the top bunk onto the floor. He took the full force of the fall. She landed on top of him with her forearm accidentally hitting him in the throat breaking his neck and killing him instantly. Law enforcement had been looking for this guy. He had committed other rapes. The student had taken the self-defense course for enjoyment and didn't take the training that seriously. Later she got in contact with the trainer to tell him the story and how thankful she was to have learned what she did. She was not prosecuted, in fact, the police applauded her for her actions.

Risk Analysis R

Risk analysis, as it pertains to self-defense, means taking the time to learn how to recognize key signs that allow you to predict the probability of a threat materializing in order to eliminate or mitigate that risk. Prior knowledge of the inherent risks in any situation allows you to prepare and manage those risks. Knowledge is power, if acted upon. Do the research.

Consider this: You are paddling your canoe down a river. Up ahead you notice a large mist looming above the river. You hear the roar of what sounds like crashing water and in the distance, you see tree-tops and sky. Odds are you are heading for a waterfall, right? Maybe it's time to paddle to shore and portage around the hazard. Doing nothing means you will find yourself frantically back-paddling your ass off with the front end of your canoe hanging over the abyss. Better yet, do the research and study the map to know that there are three waterfalls and a total drop of 285 feet on this stretch of the river before getting in that water. Or one can opt for ignorance and chance and let nature weed out the reckless from amongst us.

Or maybe you go to a closed-door of a room in your basement where you keep a trash container. In this case a larg drum made of cardboard. You notice the slight smell of smoke as you also notice what looks like smoke drifting along the top and bottom cracks of the door. You decide not to open the door and immediately call the fire department. The firefighters arrive. One goes in the side door and down the stairs to the door of the room, another waits just outside the side door of the house on the cement porch which is three feet above the driveway. The firefighter in the basement stands in front of the unopened door. In the room were smoldering ashes in the trash from a fireplace cleaning a few hours earlier, that are now superheated materials deprived of oxygen. The firefighter opens the door which allowed fresh oxygen to enter, which, if you know a little about combustibles, you realize caused an explosion. It blew the doors off the house and catapulted the outside firefighter 5 feet backward off the porch landing on his back in the driveway. Interestingly the firefighter that opened the door just got his hat blown off. The house caught fire taking out that basement room and the kitchen above it. We spent three weeks in a hotel during the remodel. Had my father not done some risk assessment and heeded the warning signs we probably would have lost the house and maybe life.

Early threat detection allows an early response but to see things early, while they are still small, we have to be paying attention. We have to be aware using our eyes, ears and all of our Spidey senses. Earbuds, eyes looking down, distractions, alcohol and drugs numb our senses leaving us vulnerable. The goal is not to be an easy target. We want to become unnoticeable or noticed in a good way, as a very bad choice for victimization.

What does danger look like? We can call upon our own experiences from when we were younger. Where we were trusting and taken advantage of and possibly hurt. We can also learn from others' experiences. Talk to people who have been where you are going or have done what you are going to do. Ask people if they have been in harrowing situations if they might be willing to discuss how they got through it or what they might do differently. When you hear about crime, think of how you might react in the same situation. Run scenarios through your mind. As you train and grow so do your capabilities. Some things that used be threats no longer will be. Some things that used to scare you won't anymore. You are no longer a child so easily fooled. You are not delicate or broken, you are skeptical, capable and a force to be recorded with.

Risk takes many forms. Vehicles for example. In 2017, a male subject deliberately drove his car into a crowd of people who were peacefully protesting, killing one and injuring 28. In 2014, a car plowed into seven after a fight broke out at, of all things, a birthday party.

Some cities are installing barricade systems to help prevent deadly vehicle assaults. Let's be honest, is this something you even consider when out in public? It's hard to prepare for everything but being informed and using situation awareness will reduce risk.

High risk areas:

- when alone
- low lit areas
- parking lots
- in your home
- elevators
- 24-hour tellers
- community parks
- amusement parks
- X-rated areas
- strip clubs
- hangouts for drug deals
- dilapidated buildings

Behavioral high risk:

- escalating anger
- increased volume

- emotional conversations
- someone moving too close
- the presence of drugs or alcohol

If you see a weapon, obviously the risk and fear factor just went through the roof.

Hands

Always check the hands for weapons. If one or both hands are concealed, be aware that the person may be hiding a weapon.

Uninvited Touch

If someone moves into your space and puts their hands on you in any unwelcomed manner, don't hesitate to communicate your discomfort. You can do this by recoiling, creating some distance and looking at them with disapproval. If they approach again, you raise your protective wall (hands up, The Fence) and communicate your desire for them to keep their distance. If they persist it's time for more active, and possibly aggressive self-defense.

Everyone is a potential threat until they aren't. People pass by you and continue on? They aren't a threat today. Tomorrow they notice you taking the same route? They may be a threat today or in the future. They have discovered something about you and your routine that they can use.

Your Call Y

Your call means that you and only you get to decide what actions you will take in the practice of your self-defense. Only you know the situation you may face and what options you may perceive at the time. We hope to be prudent so we don't win in the streets only to lose in court. In legal proceedings, you will be judged on the reasonableness of your actions (called the reasonable man theory). A jury of twelve will decide if your interpretation of events and response was reasonable and proportional to the threat. There's an old adage that says, "when in doubt, it's better to be judged by twelve than carried by six." If you honestly fear jeopardy, great bodily harm, sexual assault or death you are generally pretty safe doing what you feel is necessary to secure your safety. Once, however, a threat no longer exists, you are legally obligated to disengage and not to pursue your own assault on them.

The Victory Model Quick Reference Guide to Self Defense

Victory Model
COMMUNICATION AND BOUNDARIES
FOR SELF-DEFENSE

Visual
Body language including stances, postures, movements, and gestures. Be relaxed, confident and observant, not jittery, frightened, or oblivious. See: Non-Victim Profile/Victim Profile. (55% of communication - visual)

Communication skills

Intonation
Manner of utterance: tone, pace, soft, hard, loud, quiet, calm, anxious. Sounding off - a loud shout. Confident, powerful. Big. A high-five. Commanding tone. (Voice weapon) (38% of communication - our voice)

Content
What you say; the words you use. Congruency is believability (must match V&I above) A few words well spoken – Be direct, not talkative. Command language. Asking questions engage the mind. • You need to step back 5 ft. • I don't think so • Get back • You are making me feel uncomfortable and you need to stop • Stop right there • Back off • Yell "Someone is assaulting me call 911" (7% of communication - words)

Territory
Setting and maintaining boundaries. Space: Public 6 – 12 ft. Private 3 - 6 ft. Intimate (perfume range) inside 3-ft. and is by permission only. Stand firm in your resolve to protect this zone.

Techniques

Orientation for **O**ptimization
Position the mind and body for your best chances. Neutralize an assailant's effort and enhance yours; off-line, hands up, open hands, in close, cover their right side, left hand and foot forward. Strategic positioning is required for any scenario. Weapons proficiency, whether offence or defense requires training.

Considerations
Multiple attackers
Assailant's mental state
Size of the attacker

Risk Analysis
The ability to assess a threat, real or perceived, for an effective, response. To use lethal force in response to a potential threat you must be able to articulate that the attacker had the means, opportunity and intent to do you grave bodily harm.

Weapons threat
Low level options
Opportunity to flee
Your capabilities
Lethal threat = means, opportunity & intent for jeopardy

Your Call (no guarantees)
Your actions and their consequences are your responsibility. Knowledge, experience and training increase your options in choosing a reasonable and victorious response when confronting a potential threat. Consult your instincts but trust your training; if it's good training.

Better to be judged by 12 than to be carried by 6.

Mirandette's Martial Arts ©

Chapter 5
SAFE PRACTICES

Safe practices are things we do that lessen our vulnerability. They are risk reduction strategies that we utilize. That means to act on, to implement, to build into our lives and routines, not just think about. It's active and it takes some effort. It always starts with knowledge and awareness. Knowledge for instance: It's useful to know that the vast majority of homicides committed in the U.S. each year are committed by handguns. (according to FBI UCR'S Uniform Crime Reports latest data - 2016) Knives account for the second largest category of homicides. Blunt objects (clubs, hammers, etc.) and personal weapons (hands, fists, feet, etc.) both, individually, account for more homicides than rifles.

Guns

It might not have occurred to you that if someone were to pull a gun on you, one option may be simply to run. Of course, that option requires the right conditions and you being ready to act. You would need a path of escape, the ability to run, meaning physically and also circumstantially where you are not leaving others behind. You would hope that after losing control of the situation the assailant would see no benefit in shooting at an increasingly small and moving target. Hopefully you could run for cover and or concealment. Cover will stop a bullet. Concealment hides you but won't stop a bullet. In a mall, signage and plants will hide you. Stone pillars and large concrete planters filled with dirt will stop a bullet. Rule number one in a shooting situation is to improve your position if you are able. Move, move, move. You will be less likely to get hit if shot at.

Consider these statistics from independent agencies who study officer shooting rates and accuracy: Police officer shooting accuracy, in deadly force encounters, using the weapon they are trained on, is anywhere between 17% and 52%.

That is as low as one in five bullets hitting the target. Many factors affect shooting accuracy, e.g., time of day, amount of light, quality of training (yours and theirs), if people are shooting back, the possibility of more than one threat and one's experience. A moving target is harder to hit—so maybe you move. If you do get shot, do not assume that the wound will be fatal. Gunshot victims, contrary to popular belief, have a fairly high rate of survival, assuming that they do not take the round directly to a vital organ, for instance, the heart or brain. Dr. Vincent J.M. DiMaio, former chief medical examiner in Bexar County, Texas, and author of "Gunshot Wounds," states that you have as high as a 95% chance of survival if you get to the hospital while your heart is still beating.

(Taken from Gunshot Wounds – Practical aspects of firearms, ballistics, and forensic techniques by Vincent J.M. DiMaio, Copywrite © 1993 by CRC Press LLC - Second Edition, Boca Raton Florida, CRC Press LLC, 1999)

If you realize that you have been shot, you need to get medical attention as soon as possible. Call 911. You also need to stop the bleeding as blood loss is what kills most people in this circumstance. Locate the bleeding and apply pressure or fasten a tourniquet high and tight to an affected limb.

If an attacker orders you to get into a car, in an attempted abduction, do everything possible, if given the opportunity, not to comply. It is generally considered best practice to resist and take your chances where you are instead of going to a secluded secondary crime scene.

Knife

A quick rule of thumb that I teach kids, to anchor the point of not trying to disarm an assailant or fight the weapon is: If you see a gun run. If you see a knife, run for your life. Of course, of course, again, you only run if it's reasonable and you believe will better your position and doesn't put you in greater jeopardy. Knife attacks happen up close. It's so important that you have active situational awareness and protect your personal space. If you see that an assailant has a knife or suspect that they do, consider immediately increasing distance between you and the threat, if, you have the range to do so. Move away. Put something between you and the attacker, anything. If you have the opportunity, run and yell to draw attention to yourself. Don't think that you can take a knife away from someone. Movies depict the hero standing their ground, performing some fancy disarming technique on a knife-wielding attacker to save the day and they never seem to get cut or maybe they're cut just enough to look tough for dramatic affect. In reality, knife wounds are terrible. If you have a strong stomach research knife wounds and surviving edged weapons sometime.

The very first thing I teach in defending against a knife is: expect to get cut. You may not feel it. Victims of knife wounds said that they were shocked to feel their own warm blood running down their bodies. There are a few, pretty nice, knife defense techniques, including blocks, counters and disarms but this takes training, lots of training, and even then, there are no guarantees. I won't address that training in this book. The only thing I will say is run if possible, negotiate if you can and fight if you have no other choice. And don't think knife fighting is anything other than hell.

Having stated the above, let me tell you a success story. I was instructing at a 3-day martial arts summer camp at a college. A woman who I will refer to as Kim, approached me asking if I could teach her knife fighting. I said sure. She pulled out a razor-sharp, double-edged dagger that she wanted to use for the lesson. I said I would be happy to train her but let's put the sheath on for safety. She said, "I want it to be realistic." I said, Yes, but I don't want to get cut. We worked on skills for the next couple of days and then parted ways. A few weeks later she sent me a thank you letter along with a news clipping and a policer report. The article described a woman who successfully repelled a knife wielding attacker with her martial arts.

Kim told me that she got out of work, went to her car and got in. A man rose up from the back seat and put a knife to her throat. (Now, that's got to be one of the scariest things that can happen to someone, right?). She thought for a second and then did a move to get the knife off of her throat, grabbed for the door handle, opened the door and got out of the car. He got out from the back seat and lunged at her with the knife. She blocked his attack and hit him. He lunged again, she parried and knocked him into the bushes. He then, ran away. Her willingness and training paid off. Kim decided to resist and not allow her attacker to force her to drive to a secondary crime scene where she would have been isolated and at greater risk.

Exits

Have a contingency plan. In any building, home, open-air venue, fenced-in area, parking lot, airplane, ship, elevator, subway, or highway, there are ways in and ways out. There are exits and emergency exits, front doors and back doors, trap doors, maintenance access doors and windows. Knowing where they are gives you a possible escape route should you need it. If a threat comes through the front door or an exit is blocked, you are moving toward an alternative exit. When in public, I always sit facing the door if possible.

Safe Spaces

Safe spaces are areas that are safer than others because of the inherent protection it offers from an assailant. It used to be, until this year, it seems, that if you were around people, in public, in the middle of the day, or in well-lit areas, you felt pretty safe from harassment, assault, robbery, rape or being killed. But in this current climate, in 2021, some criminals riot, loot, terrorize and are emboldened to commit crimes almost anywhere and anytime thinking no one will stop them. Today, more than ever, you have to be responsible for your own protection and BYOB.

For personal crime to happen to you physically, unless it involves a projectile, someone has to get close to you. Anytime you *notice* someone is paying an inordinate amount of attention to you or approaching, you need to be able to quickly activate a plan to move to a better position and greater safety. Remember. Distance equals time. Time gives us more options.

If someone is getting too close, put your hands up, step back, establish some distance and reestablish it you have to. In the book "No More Fear" author Stephen M. Thompson advises that if someone is bothering you in a social setting and trying to make conversation, a good rule of thumb is to <u>decrease interaction time and increase distance</u>. If approached, don't feel obligated to answer any questions, for instance; "Do you smoke?" "Do you come here often?" "What's your name?" Or. "What are you drinking?" You can politely say, excuse me, and walk away. If you're walking on the street and approached by a street person or beggar and don't want to be hassled, ignore them and keep walking or say simply "sorry" and keep walking. Do not engage them in conversation unless that is your choice. (No More Fear by Steven Thompson. Copywrite © 1987 Kendall/Hunt Publishing Company, ISBN: 0840344503, ISBN13: 9780840344502)

<u>Notice What Others Miss</u>

Do you notice how light reflects off a windshield onto the walls or ceiling of your home at certain times of the day? Do you notice motion in reflective surfaces at home, work or wherever you spend time? Do you notice air pressure changes when a door or window is opened and closed? Notice how floors and stairs creak when walked on and how it differs depending on the persons weight?

When I was in Japan touring an ancient castle, we walked across large wood-planked floors called "nightingale floors" that squeaked and chirped as we stepped from board to board. That was by design as part of their security system. They were not fastened together but were made to flex and rub against one another and squeak. That is why ninjas walked on walls and ceilings, to avoid making noise.

Early warnings are better than late. Our environment is talking and giving us valuable information. Are we listening?

<u>The Bodyguard</u>

If you decided to become a professional bodyguard, the first thing you would learn is that your absolute number one responsibility is the safety and well-being of your client. This training involves many hours of research and planning to avoid and overcome any potential risk or critical failure points that could be encountered where you are, where you're going and anywhere in-between. You have to plan for the who, what, where, when and how of a hostile's possible actions. Above all the intel gathering and preparation, you have to be willing to put yourself at risk in a worst-case scenario as the last line of defense. Meaning, you have to be willing to sacrifice yourself for the client if necessary; you "take the bullet," so to speak, figuratively and literally.

You are your own bodyguard - be a good one. Take the principles in this book seriously and take a martial arts or self-defense course. What, where, when, how and from who might your client be vulnerable?

Don't be predictable. Whether on a college campus, going to work or the grocery store, plan your route and vary it. Look for your soft spots and blind spots (areas of vulnerability, chinks in your armor, a place from where someone could pounce). Pretend that you are the attacker planning to attack you. Your job is to gather information on you, analyze it and rate where you are most vulnerable. Would it be a dorm hallway, near your car, in your room, at the office, at home? If the attacker knew as much about you as you do, when would he/she/they strike and what direction would the approach come from?

Whether it's a military operation, a professional bodyguard's assignment or our personal self-defense we want to determine our vulnerability, which includes where the attack is coming from. In his book "Sheep No More" Jonathan T. Gilliam calls this direction the "avenue of approach." Gilliam in making a comparison between humans and the animal kingdom says this, "Animals on the plains of Africa don't just react to fear as experienced 'experts' would have you believe. Instead, prey animals that live daily under intense threats of larger, faster predators develop an understanding of which areas around them are critically dangerous, the critical times those areas present the biggest threat, and the location and direction for tactical avenues of approach a predator will likely take when they attack. These prey animals also have an in-depth, instinctual understanding of who the attackers are and what their own vulnerabilities are compared to their enemies' strengths. They are constantly learning from their parents and through their own experiences, then applying it to their overall knowledge of defense and responsive actions…."

Predator and prey are involved in a daily, lifelong practice of utilizing learned, taught and instinctual knowledge, both offensive and defensive, to survive. Those that learn best and fastest live longer.

(Sheep No More – The Art of Awareness and Attack Survival by Jonathan T. Gilliam. Copywrite © 2017 by Jonathan T. Gilliam. Post Hill Press Publisher. ISBN 978-1-68261-604-8 ISBN)

Do you drive in isolated areas? Vigilance is everything. Incorporate safe practices. Don't chance running out of gas, EVER. Nick Hughes, author of "Be Your Own Bodyguard," recommends your car's new empty is half full. If you ever have to drive your way out of trouble don't want your gas tank reading 1/8th full (7/8th empty). When you get to half a tank, fill up. Keep your vehicle in good working order.

Thankfully predators don't know us as well as we do and don't know our blind spots (vulnerabilities). Keep it that way. Our personal information and routines are sacred and need to be kept private. Be strategic and protect it.

<u>Your Visual Perceptual Range</u>

You can push out your perceptual range and check for threats. This is where you intentionally force your vision in and out to different distances to see what otherwise might get missed. One defense agency and some military branches use the rule of 0 - 5 - 15- and 50-meter concentric zones of safety. Zero - is there something where I'm standing that can kill me? How about 5 meters away? 15? And so on. Force yourself to scan these concentric circles (a 360-degree view) for danger, 0, 5, 15 and 50 meters out.

<u>Splash Vision</u>

Another useful visual method of detecting a threat is called splash vision*. Cats and other animals use it by holding a steady gaze in the direction of interest and then noticing anything that *moves* in their field of vision. You react to seeing movement from non-movement quicker than movement from movement. Test this out yourself sometime. Look at a scene or landscape that is still and observe how any new motion is immediately detectable. There is a game that uses this exact principle. It's called Wak-A-Mole. You put your money in, pick up the mallet, steady your gaze over 5 holes in a table and wait. When a mole pokes his little head out of a hole you smack him back down. In the movie "The Bodyguard" Kevin Costner is chasing after a killer in the woods outside of a cabin, at night, in winter. He loses sight of the guy who stopped for a moment. Keven has no idea which way to pursue so he kneels in the snow, his gun at the ready closes his eyes and listens. The killer makes a sound, Keven immediately turns and shoots in that direction. Although audible, it's the same idea as splash vision.

*Roy Harvey – Discussion of Splash Vision - Defensive Tactics Group - Splash Vision

Chapter 6
INTUITION AND INSTINCT

Our intuition can provide an early warning to danger, increasing our chances of survival, if, we listen to our gut, those feelings that are hard to describe, those times when you say, "Hmm, I can't put my finger on it but something isn't right here." Later you may say, "I knew it! I just felt something was wrong." If we learn to heed the warning signs, we better our chances.

Ben, a fellow defense instructor of mine, had a co-worker who arrived home after work, walked into her house and noticed that something didn't *feel* right. Being cautious, she immediately left the house and called him. He lived close and they had talked about the subject of safety before. He went over to investigate. They slowly walked through the house. When they went into the bathroom and drew back the shower curtain, they found candy wrappers on the floor of the shower. Someone had been waiting for her to come home and enter the bathroom. Fortunately, she paid attention to her intuition and acted on her own behalf. After that incident, she did a serious home security assessment and took measures to fortify her home.

The most important function of intuition is prediction. Because we recognize something, consciously or unconsciously, we can anticipate danger and formulate defense strategies prior to an event playing out. Our intuitive processes are habit-forming. Those habits may serve us, but maybe not. For instance: If every time I see a snake I'm debilitated because I'm subconsciously reminded of a terrifying childhood experience, that doesn't serve me well. But intuition can be trained. We can modify old instructions and press into new attitudes and responses. However, the mind is inherently lazy, says researcher and author Danial Kahneman Author of Thinking Fast Thinking Slow. Good decision making takes deliberate, reasoned thought and effort so quick decisions, based on emotion and impulse, don't win out. We need to pay attention to our gut instincts but check them to see they are beneficial in the long run. (Thinking Fast Thinking Slow, Danial Kahneman, Farrar, Strauis and Giroux Publisher, October 2011)

Albert Einstein has many quotes on the value of intuition and imagination and how they fuel discovery. You can read some of his conversation on intuition, fantasy and intellect in his book. "Out of My Later Years" (Out of My Later Years by Albert Einstein, Copywrite © 1956 by Publisher Citadel Press, ISBN 0806503572, 9780806503578)

Instinct is reactionary. Instinct come from the oldest part of our brains or neurological development and, again, serves as part of our primal survival mechanism. Instincts are processed and controlled by the limbic system (our old brain - amygdala) which can bypass, or hijack, the cerebral system (our thinking brain – neocortex). Imbedded instructions in our brains cause unconscious reactions like pulling back from a hot stove or quick movement to hearing a sudden, loud noise. It triggers our fight or flight response. According to Daniel Goleman, author of "Emotional Intelligence," who coined the phrase emotional hijack or amygdala hijack, "The amygdala can take control over what we do even as the thinking brain, the neocortex, is still coming to a decision...... This puts the amygdala in a powerful post in mental life, something like a psychological sentinel challenging every situation, every perception, with but one kind of question in mind, the most primitive, 'Is this something I hate? That hurts me? Something I fear?' if so-if the moment at hand somehow draws a 'yes' – the amygdala reacts instantaneously, like a neural tripwire, telegraphing a message of crisis to all parts of the brain." The prospect may be, am I going to have lunch or be lunch. We experience the fight flight or freeze.

(Emotional Intelligence by Danial Goleman, Copywrite © 1995 by Danial Goleman Publisher Bantam Dell a division of Random House, Inc. ISBN-13: 978-0-553-80491-1, ISBN-10:0-553-80491-X)

Fight, Flight or Freeze - Understanding
your autonomic nervous system

We've all experienced the fight-or-flight (or freeze) reaction after being frightened or surprised.

A fight or flight response to varying degrees of stress and danger may be useful for our safety or survival but freezing up and doing nothing, like the preverbal deer in the headlights, probably isn't the best option, if we have a choice. And we do.

How do we deal with freezing up; the paralysis that can accompany fear and critical incident stress? It's helpful to understand some of the physiological effects of stress so we can prepare and perform under those conditions.

Your sympathetic nervous system (SNS) takes over when the brain perceives a deadly force threat. It affects us in many or all of the following ways:

- Thinking stops
- Perceptual distortions
- Auditory exclusion—diminished ability to hear
- Tunnel vision— (reduced peripheral field)
- Slow-motion time (things seem to happen in slow motion)
- Loss of fine motor and complex motor skills
- Rapid heart-beat
- Adrenalin release increasing strength
- Liver releases glucose to improve energy for muscles
- And more

SNS dominance is catastrophic to three systems: vision, cognitive processing and fine and complex motor skill performance. Gross motor skill is all that is left, according to researchers, one of whom is Lt. Col. Dave Grossman.

In a story; an old master was with his disciple walking in the woods when they observed a rabbit being chased by a fox. The student observed that it would not be long before the hare would be caught and eaten by the faster, and probably smarter, fox.

The master replied that this particular rabbit would get away and that they should stay and watch. Sure enough, after 5 minutes of watching, the rabbit did get away, leaving a tired and hungry fox. The student was impressed with his master's knowledge and asked him to explain how he knew. The master smiled and answered: the fox was running for his dinner. The rabbit was running for his life.

The amygdala hijack reaction, as I stated, can be beneficial if it gets us clear of danger by formulating an immediate plan and acting on it but it can also be very inconvenient and even dangerous when it prevents us from doing what's needed to save our lives in high-stakes situations. Is there a way to interrupt or hinder this reaction?

Managing Arousal in High Stakes Situations

Stress alters performance. In his book "On Combat", Lt. Col. Dave Grossman, former West Point psychology professor, professor of military science and Army Ranger, author and expert on the effects of stress in combat say this: "Stress Inoculation - performance under stress: both cognitive performance and complex motor skills, like throwing a football and aiming a gun are at their peak between 115 and 145 bpm (beats per minute) heart rate. When heart rates go above 175 bpm, capacity for all skilled tasks disintegrates and individuals begin to experience catastrophic cognitive and physical breakdown. By knowing how stress impacts their performance in life-or-death situations, warriors can take steps to help mitigate its effects either through training or stress-management techniques."

(On Combat by Lt. Col. Dave Grossman & Loren W. Christensen, Copywrite © 2008, Human Factor Research Group, Inc. and Warrior Science Publications. Materials used with permission from Lt. Col. Grossman.)

Following are just a few techniques used by military personnel, martial artists, performers, yoga students, public speakers and others to better perform under stress:

1. Tactical breathing, sometimes called 4 by 4 breathing.
   By physically controlling your breathing, you can change your physiology, helping to calm down and stay focused. Here is how it works:

   1. Slowly inhale a deep breath for 4 seconds
   2. Hold the breath in for 4 seconds
   3. Slowly exhale the breath for 4 seconds
   4. Hold the empty breath for 4 seconds
   5. Repeat until your breathing is under control and your heart rate under 145 bpm.

2. Pre-think it
   We can run scenarios in our minds of high-stress situations with potential responses. This will also improve response time.

   Recognize that it takes time to go from perception to action even when you anticipate the danger. Because action beats reaction we must plan and stay aware to minimize that response time.

   Bruce Siddle's research measures reaction time in four stages. (Bruce Siddle – Author of many books including Sharpening the Warriors Edge, founder of the PPCT – Pressure Point Control Tactics)

   • It takes at least .25 seconds to *perceive* a problem
   • It takes at least .25 seconds to *evaluate* the problem
   • It takes at least .25 seconds to *select* a response
   • It takes at least .25 seconds to *initiate* the response (depending on the response selected)

   Even when measuring athletes who are in top physical form, in some tests, it took at least a full second before any response was able to be executed not including any hesitation. It's good to have a plan but Dr. R. A. Solomon (contributor to law enforcement traumatic reactions research) states how things don't always go to plan and the real response might just be:

- Oh s—!
- Welcome to HELL!
- Survive
- React

Everyone can be surprised or shocked, but sometimes winning or survival depends on how quickly we can regain a degree of composure to take action. Self-regulation takes discipline and practice.

3. Task relevant self-talk
    To mitigate or counter the detrimental effects of stress, talk out loud to yourself as if you were in training. Repeat commands so you remember them. Police are trained to say, "Get down on the ground." and "Let me see your hands.", repeatedly so they will say it when it matters and tensions are high. The subject needs to hear commands over and over loudly for other reasons. They themselves are experiencing high anxiety auditory exclusion; they are not hearing you. Maybe it's because of the flash bang that just went off or the forced entry with armed police running in or fear of their pending arrest, but commands, many times, need to be repeated to get compliance.

4. Acronyms
    In shooting schools, instructors program their members to use the acronyms TRR and TRS in remembering what to do for a pistol malfunction. TRR means tap, rack, ready. TRS is tap, rack, shoot. One is for a shooting situation, the other is for a potential shooting situation. You tap the bottom of the magazine to make sure it's seated (locked securely), rack to chamber a new round, clearing the potential failure and then you are ready to shoot.

The acronym BRASS is an easy way to remember the shooting process. Breathe, Relax, Aim, Sight, Squeeze.

This same memory method was used by a very nervous bride-to-be who was standing at the back of the church as the music started. Her mother said "Honey all you have to do is focus on getting down the aisle, to the altar and him. Just say aisle - altar - him to yourself repeatedly." As she walked, she was heard saying, "I'll alter him, I'll alter him." A joke. But the concept is sound. Simple verbal prompts help us focus.

Blind Spots

Your eye does have actual blind spots where the retina has no photoreceptors but for our purposes, blind spots are defined as areas of undetected, potential hazard or vulnerability; places where you can be taken off guard or blind-sided. It's the "I never saw it coming," or "It happened so fast. He came out of nowhere." Blind spots can also be attitudinal. For example: "I don't go bad places so I don't worry about being assaulted." Let me use a driving analogy to describe the concept for our self-defense.

In driver's education, we were taught to always check the blind spot before changing lanes. This means looking back over your shoulder into the lane near your back fenders to see if there is a vehicle there that your mirrors aren't picking up. While in college, two of my good friends were in serious car accidents because they did just that. They took their eyes off the road to make a "head check," which only took a second, but in that short time, they put themselves in peril by not being able to react quickly enough to avoid plowing into the vehicle that unexpectedly stopped in front of them.

Driving at 70 mph, you travel 102 feet per second. If a head check takes a second, and it takes another second to see and react to what is happening in front of you. That's 204 feet of road that you have no control over. You don't have time to react to avoid an accident should something happen in front of you. Two hundred and four feet! That's two-thirds of a football field. Now add wet, or icy road conditions and the results just get worse.

While driving my car I recognized that, if my mirrors were set correctly, I could see 360 degrees around me without taking my eyes off the road in front of me. Engineers at a well-known automotive mirror manufacturing company, that I used to work for, confirmed that mirrors are designed to give us a complete view around our car and eliminate blind spots; if they are used correctly.

Why do we point all three mirrors on our car in the same direction -backward? (see Figure A) Because people need a reference point to locate themselves visually with other vehicles on the road. We know where our rear fenders are so that view is comfortable even though most of that view is available in the rearview mirror. And comfort is key when surrounded by speeding, heavy metal objects. The problem is it's dangerous. You are not able to safely and quickly change lanes without looking back first. The solution: find a new reference point. Here's how: set your mirrors out 10 to 15 degrees from where they are now, out from the rear fender (see Figure B). Sitting straight in the driver's seat, you now see an undefined area in your side view mirrors but, lay your left ear toward your left shoulder while looking in your left mirror and you can then see your rear fender again. Lay your right ear on your right shoulder to see your back fender to set your ride side mirror. To check and see if they're set right, while driving, let a car pass you on your left. First, you can see them in the rearview mirror. They leave that view and you can now clearly see them in your side view mirror (formerly the blind spot). They leave that mirror and you can now pick them up in your peripheral vision while not taking your eyes off the road in front. Then, pass that car and reverse the sequence seeing them in front, right peripheral, side view mirror and rearview mirror again. You are now set for optimal driving efficiency with 360° vision. You can quickly change lanes without taking your eyes off the road in front of you.

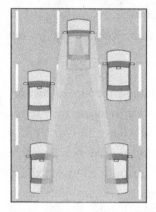

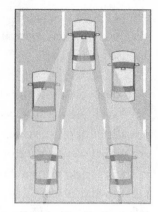

| Figure A | Figure B |

Some people resist change even when they know it makes sense to do so. The CEO of a company said to me, after a seminar, "I know you are right but it's too uncomfortable for me, at this point, to change." He will continue in his familiar way of driving and accept the risk. If we are willing to modify our routines to incorporate risk reduction strategies, we will improve our safety quotient (a measure of vulnerability).

Reference points help us evaluate, compare and navigate. They make our lives easier. We use them every day in a hundred ways. In self-defense, our point of reference, as far as our mindset, needs to start with: "Can't touch this!

OODA LOOP

John Boyd, USAF fighter pilot and pentagon consultant, put together the acronym OODA to describe that which all of us do, every day, many times a day, and sometimes, many times per minute. It describes the 4 stages of thought from observation, that which we perceive to be happening, to the action we take in response, based on our objective. Col. Boyd's objective was more than just air superiority, it was survival. He is credited with revolutionizing our militaries (fighter aircraft) aerial tactics and more. Those of us who saw the movie Top Gun got to see a little of Col. Boyd's aerial strategy performed when Maverick, engaged in air to air combat, in his F-18 Super Hornet said "I'm gonna hit the brakes, he'll fly right by." After which, the enemy found himself in a vulnerable position.

His OODA model is useful for us to understand in optimizing our self-defense capabilities.

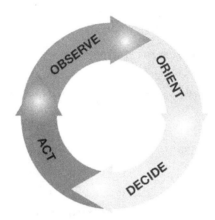

OODA LOOP, like the Victory Model, is a quick guide to help us organize our thinking to make decisions faster than the other guy.

O - Observe

Observation means to gather information to see if a situation requires our attention.

O - Orient

This is how we position or adjust our mind and body to attain the objective. In Boyd's words, "We filter information through our cultural traditions, generic heritage and previous experience along with any new information, and that shapes the way we observe, the way we orient and the way we act. In other words, who we are and where we come from influences the way we process information and make decisions."

(Boyd, John, R. Col., The Essence of Winning and Losing, June 28th, 1995 – slide presentation.)

D – Decide

We choose an option.

A - Act

Execute the chosen course of action.

LOOP means to circle back to Observe. As soon as one cycle is complete, another scenario presents itself, and then another. We have to be nimble in mind and body to quickly outmaneuver others whether an enemy, assailant or competition.

Here is the secret, in self-defense tactics, to what is called, getting inside the other guy's OODA, where you get to your endgame before the enemy gets to theirs. The would-be attacker has a plan, a script that he hopes to carry out. He has the advantage and the element of surprise. He's counting on you being discombobulated. People are frequently distracted, unaware of their surroundings (Cooper's color white).

If you can detect that you are being targeted for exploitation early enough, you can change the script, do the unexpected and gain the advantage. After his plan has been disrupted, he has to readjust, reformulate and decide if it's worth continuing. He is back in his OODA. You are carrying out yours.

OODA can happen many times in a few seconds or take minutes even hours. Example: A battleship shoots a warning shot over another ship's bow (put one over the bow, as it were) then waits to see what the response is before their next move. Another example: A 12-year-old girl was walking into a high school football game with her father, lagging a few yards behind him. An older teen rushed up to her and grabbed her coat, trying to steal it. She yelled to her dad but he didn't hear her over the fan noise. She was a karate student so she tried to block his hands away but that didn't work. We are now into her third loop in as many seconds. She threw a kick to his groin squarely connecting, causing him to let go. She then ran and caught up to her dad. If the first option doesn't work, move to the next and then the next. Things don't always go as planned. Or may I say, never go as planned.

I added AN to OODA which lengthens the acronym but shortens the loop. It stands for Anticipate. ANOODA. We can anticipate based on our experience and intuition which allows for sharper observation and quicker response. Just remember that effective responses require training. Get some.

Air Force Colonel John Boyd

Besides the OODA Loop model, here are some things Col. Boyd is known for.

- He flew the F-86 Sabre Jet in Korea.
- Formulated the Aerial Attack Study which revolutionized aerial tactics.
- Helped Dick Chaney plan the invasion of Iraq, Desert Storm (left hook design).
- He's credited for largely developing the strategy for the invasion of Iraq in the Gulf War of 1991. Desert Shield (Desert Storm's fighting phase of the conflict).
- Often referred to as the greatest military strategist in history that no one knows.

Chapter 7
LEGALLY SPEAKING

Legal Considerations and Protections

In Michigan and 44 other states, at this time, there are strong legal protections called CSC Laws (Criminal Sexual Conduct), for unwanted sexual touch and rape (Michigan's penal code Act 328 of 1931 Chapter LXXVI Section 750.520). Check the laws in your state and jurisdiction for legal interpretations and recourse to sexual assault.

Sexual assault is defined, in general, as any form of unwanted sexual contact obtained without consent and/or obtained through the use of force, threat of force, intimidation or coercion. Touching can be considered sexual assault, even the touching of clothing over intimate areas, depending on the circumstances.

<u>Stand Your Ground Law</u>

In Michigan, we have a stand your ground law (MCL 780.972), originally called "self-defense act" and referred to as "castle doctrine." It states that a person does not have the duty to retreat if he or she honestly and reasonably believes the use of deadly force is necessary to prevent imminent great bodily harm, sexual assault or death to themselves or others. There's a two-pronged test for a person to use deadly force. They have to actually believe their actions are preventing great bodily harm, sexual assault or death, also, that belief has to be objectively reasonable under the circumstances. In other words, would 12 people decide they would have done what you did, or more, in the same circumstances? This became law in 2006. Stand your ground expanded the castle doctrine (Castle - in our home or castle) to anywhere you have a legal right to be; car, home, office, etc.

Again, check the laws in your state. Many states have a "castle doctrine" that removes the necessity to flee before using deadly force, but are very specific as to the location.

Acceptable Use of Force when considering self-defense

In my classes, I present a scenario of a potential assault and then ask a question. The response I get is always the same. See how you would answer.

You are a normal, well-adjusted, 40-year-old woman minding your own business when from across the room a person, a male, approaches you with a menacing look on his face. He is definitely heading straight at you. He has a big knife in his hand. About 6 feet away he says, "I'm going to kill you dead." He is between you and the only exit and there are no other people near to intervene.

The Question: Are you justified, at this point, in using an aggressive physical attack to protect yourself? If you have a gun within reach, can you use it? Male subject, aggressive demeanor, knife in his hand, verbally threatens great bodily harm, in close proximity. Your answer?

Most people answer yes. The answer is: It depends.

Consider now that this perpetrator is only 4 years old. He is wearing a little red cape. The knife is a, plastic sword. He is playing superhero and he has picked you to be the villain.

This scenario is not meant to make light of assault but to make a point. In deciding what degree of force would be considered appropriate in any given situation, you have to be able to articulate certain threat criteria were met.

To use the right of self-defense, legally, the threat has to be real and believable. The amount and degree of force which may be employed to defend oneself will be determined by the surrounding circumstances including but not limited to:

- The age and sex of the assailant(s)
- The stature and physical condition of each
- The opportunity to flee
- The number of subjects involved
- The presence of weapons or perceived presence of weapons
- The mental state of the subjects
- The feasibility of alternative actions

In addition, the assailant must demonstrate the means, opportunity and intent to do you harm.

Means:

- A person's size, strength and skill
- The presence of a weapon - club, knife, car, brick, etc.

Opportunity:

- Proximity - close enough to carry out an attack, or for the weapon to be effective.

Intent:

- Discovered through threatening language
- Ascertained through threatening posture and body language (see Ritualized Combat - Immanent Assault Behaviors)
- A weapon sighted on you

If you perceive a threat, based on the above criteria, you have the right to defend yourself.

Every day law enforcement makes make split-second decisions that can change their lives and the lives of others forever. Shoot or not to shoot? Was the threat real? The youth reached in his pocket and spun around raising his arm toward the officer and is shot by the officer. Later it's discovered that he only had a phone in his hand. The threat doesn't have to be real but perceived as real. You can't shoot someone because you were afraid. Again, there has to be a reasonable presumption of jeopardy.

To help mitigate these tragedies, law enforcement agencies have policies that guide their use of force in resolving a subject's escalation of resistance. One such guide is called the "use of force continuum." The lowest level is usually verbal commands, however, sometimes just the officer's presence and authority or reputation can defuse a situation.

**Law Enforcement
Use of Force Continuum**

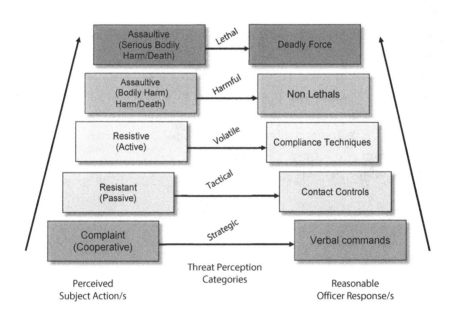

Compliance Techniques

Beyond verbal commands, compliance techniques include empty-hand controls including grabs, joint-locks and striking.

Non-lethal Measures

Non-lethal measures that police officers can use include blunt impact weapons (baton, soft projectile), chemical agents and CED (Conductive Energy Device) also known as a Taser (Taser is a brand of conductive electrical weapons sold by Axon Co.). Although categorized as non-lethal force, many deaths per year result from the use of Tasers.

Lethal Force

Lethal/deadly force describes taking action that is likely to cause great bodily harm or death.

Whereas law enforcement is accountable to agency policies and the law, we too can be prosecuted for excessive force in self-defense. We need to do only what a reasonable person would believe necessary to prevent the harm that we perceive. High emotions are taken into consideration when determining if someone acted inappropriately and with excessive force. In martial arts, we teach ability with responsibility. We want to use the least amount of force necessary to neutralize a threat. (Ref. NIJ National Institute of Justice)

Chapter 8
ADAPTIVE WEAPONS

Adaptive weapons (also referred to as field-expedient weapons) are objects the environment provides that we can use to defend by shielding or striking. It can be almost anything: a rock, stick, hat brim or book. Just think of the arsenal available in a restaurant; utensils, dinner plate, coffee cup, coffee pot, hot coffee, glass salt and pepper shakers, serving tray, pepper itself, kitchen knives, pots and pans and chairs.

You can use chopsticks and garbage can lid, car keys, snow scraper, pens pencils or how about a road flare? A flare burns as hot as 2900 degrees Fahrenheit (1600 Celsius). It's a mini flame thrower and it's legal. They burn for 15 to 30 minutes and stay lit underwater. Some even have a metal spiked tip on one end. You can put it on the road as a warning signal to other drivers. You can also hold it in your hand and use it as a self-defense weapon. You can carry one in your purse.

Imagine that you are walking alone at night and you feel you are being stalked so you pull a flare out of your purse and light it. You have just become a very undesirable target in my opinion. In my college classes, I ask the students if they have ever handled or learned to light a flare. To date, only one student said she had. She worked with first responders. Buy a package of three flares. The cost is around $6. Take one out, pop off the top and strike the flint. You can hold it or put it on the ground; super-hot molten phosphorous sulfur will drip from the lit end, so be careful.

Flares

Here's an adaptive weapon example. A woman I know was approached in a store parking lot by two youths intending on stealing her purse. She had opened her car door to put her groceries in. Her purse was on the seat. One of the kids moved in while the other watched from a few feet away. He pushed the woman against her door and reached in for the purse. She was not about to let that happen. She had a large jug of laundry detergent in her hand. She yelled, "Get away from me!" while hitting him repeatedly in the head with the jug. The guys ran off, one holding his head, the other laughing at him.

Another example. My friend, whom I will call Merrick, was managing a convenience store. An intruder came in late at night intending to rob him. Merrick grabbed his aluminum baseball bat, that he kept behind the counter, and clobbered this guy 10 or 12 times before he went down. The robber gave up and police arrived a short time later. The intruder was bruised but had no serious injuries, to my surprise.

Repurposing objects and adding them to your fighting arsenal can increase your reach, increase your striking force and shift the balance of power in your favor.

On a cautionary note: If you are the aggressor and use what's considered excessive force, you can face charges. An acquaintance of mine got into a confrontation in a bar and decided to hit the other guy in the face while holding a shot glass in his striking hand. The blow incapacitated the aggressor and it was over; except it ended up in court where he was charged with aggravated assault with a weapon. The penalty was more severe than if he had been empty-handed.

What about placing keys between your fingers? It seems everyone has learned to try and look fierce by putting keys between their fingers to look like claws. Practically speaking, keys are like little saw blades with sharp edges. Holding them in the webbing between fingers, gives you little to no control and should you hit something they will do great damage to your hand.

The best way to use keys as a weapon is to hold all the keys pointed downward so they project out of the bottom of your clenched fist. Grip them like you might picture holding an ice pick as you chip a block of ice. The motion is a hammer-fist strike, like hitting your fist on a table. It's a more natural strike than the front punch. The keys won't shift in this grip and will do enormous damage to the flesh they come in contact with; lots of DNA will be collected.

Keys

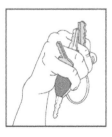   

Wrong Way   Right Way

Chapter 9
PHYSICALLY DEFENDING BOUNDARIES

For someone to physically assault you, or get their hands on you they have to get close (sometimes referred to as closing the gap). You decide to object to this encroachment and now physically enforce your boundaries. Simply put your arms out in front of you with your hands open, like you are pushing on a wall, and state what you <u>want to happen next</u>. Say, "Stop right there!" Or, maybe a gentler approach will do. You can politely say, "I'm sorry, would you mind stepping back a bit? That's a little too close for my comfort."

The Fence

No one gets to be in your intimate space without your permission. You're now in a bladed stance (one foot slightly back), with your hands up. Your weight is on your front foot and you are speaking in command language (forceful and direct). You may have tried politely asking this person to step back and now you are telling them. If they don't respect your wishes, you now know they are dangerous. You can disengage, if possible, employ other security measures or maybe proceed to a more aggressive double palm heel strike to their face or a kick to the shins. It depends on the level of threat you perceive -and your confidence in performing these moves.

Cover Block—Primal Block

The primal block is to protect you from taking blows to the head and sets up a push or strike either to get clear or counter. To cover, tuck your non-dominant hand (usually left) behind the same side ear so your arm is folded, shielding the side of your head, jaw and temple area. The second hand (right) faces outward, positioned at the elbow to intercept a straight right-hand punch. It also serves to cover the right side if needed. This defense strategy protects you while you immediately act to better your position. Sometimes that means moving into the opponent. I certainly don't advocate covering and taking blows for long.

Cover Block

Combatives

The following self-defense countermeasures involve striking and physical combat. These moves should only be used if you feel competent in executing them and when the situation warrants.

Striking

My friend, whom I will call Tony, was in New York. He was suddenly surrounded by four guys. The man directly in front of Tony had a knife aimed at Tony's midsection. The guy demanded Tony's wallet saying he wouldn't hurt him. At the same time, the knife was grazing his shirt at stomach level. Tony thought, "Sure. No problem." But then, as he reached back for his wallet, he decided, "Oh hell no!" and took a chance. He explosively threw a double palm heel strike at the guy's face knocking him backward and to the ground. Tony ran right over the top of him and down the street as the other three guys watched in surprise. The "surrounding method" of assault by these thugs made it look like just a group of friends so no attack was detected. Did Tony make the right move? In his mind, he did. He actually stepped right on the guy as he ran over him. In most cases like this, self-defense instructors would say it's recommended to turn over the money or give them the decoy wallet that has some dummy cards and small bills in it… but it's your call.

The double palm heel strike is a go-to move taught at Defensive Tactic Institute (shooting and self-defense training center) and one of my favorite no-nonsense moves.

To perform, put palms together and thrust them both forward, striking the neck and chin to force the head backward, knocking the person off balance. You can disengage here or follow-through by stepping forward and slightly to the side capturing an arm and then elbow striking the face with the other arm. The groin is also available to knee strike while stepping in. A leg sweep takedown is also available here after the elbow strike. This takes some training. (Note: The sketches that follow show striking techniques. My son and his friend, the models, thought it only fair that they both get to demonstrate. I know, it's a little weird seeing strikes demonstrated against a woman. My apologies.)

Single, double, secondary takedown

Eye Gouge

Gouging an eye causes blunt ocular trauma and possible optic nerve damage. It's uncomfortable to think about doing, but this move can be very effective in disorienting and dissuading an attack. One hand cups the back of the head while driving the thumb or fingers of the other hand into the eye. Drive it deep to the back of the eye socket, hitting the optic nerve. This is the technique that was used by the college coed defending herself against a rapist, mentioned earlier.

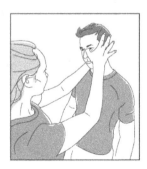 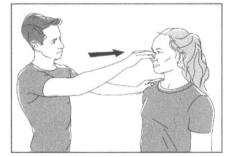

Front Choke Escape

In a front choke assault, both of the attacker's hands are around your neck. You are both standing. With his hands in this position, he is vulnerable to an attack of your own. It's absolutely necessary to get his hands off of your neck quickly as you can be rendered unconscious within seconds. At the top of the sternum, there is a soft spot between the ball ends of the clavicle bones called the clavicular notch or hyoid notch. Position your fingers like a spear, with a firm straight wrist and drive your outstretched fingers into this spot. While thrusting forward, turn your shoulders for more reach and penetration. The end position looks similar to a fencing lunge. You should be able to throw your attacker back three full steps before you turn and escape or continue your attack if you decide it's necessary. The piercing jab to his throat can also be directed at the eyes. All other karate moves against a choke, that I have seen, are inferior to this move.

Front choke escape 1, 2

Shirt Grab Escape

If someone grabs your shirt or lapels with one or two hands, immediately cover their wrist or wrists to locate, monitor and control any further actions with their hands. This is done gently like hanging a wet dishcloth over their wrists. There is no force or tension needed. Just lay your wrists over their wrists. Evaluate the threat and amount of damage you may wish to inflict and if striking is your best option. You can politely or strongly request those hands be removed while you put one foot back and lower your stance. Or, if the threat warrants, you can fire off a double palm heel strike to the upper neck and a kick to the shins or knee to the groin straight away. Be ready to launch a series of strikes driving your attacker back and to the ground, if necessary, before retreating to safety.

Weight lowered, palms move into striking position

Explosive palm-heel jolt to the upper neck and jaw driving the head back and the body off balance

Hair-Grab Escape

During an assault, if you have long hair, it's likely that it will get grabbed and pulled. This is a violent, dangerous situation. We are not as concerned about the hair as much as a neck injury (whiplash) and other damage from getting hit or shoved into something while held by the hair.

If grabbed by the hair, it's important that you quickly grab the attacker's wrist or wrists and hold his hands tightly to your head, actually pressing their hands toward your head as if they're suction cups that you are sticking to your head. At the same time put one foot back and lower your stance for balance. If you fall, it's ok; get back up if you can. You can yell, "Let go of my hair!" or try to deescalate if possible but if that doesn't work and you decide to attack you are in a very advantageous position. Launch a kick to the shin, more than once if need be. If they let go, and even if they don't, you may be able to swing your elbow over his for an arm-bar to control or to break the arm. This takes a little practice but it's effective in submitting an opponent or causing injury to the arm so they lose their grasp.

Hair-grab escape 1, 2, 3

Rear Bear Hug (Over the arms—pinning the arms)

This is a very uncomfortable position to be in. Your arms are pinned and some of your weapons are inaccessible (biting and knee strikes); or so you think. Actually, you have many good fighting options depending on your level of training. Some fighting options are as follows:

– Head butt to the face or clavicle (Figure 1)
 Even a taller attacker must bend down to capture and pin your arms. In doing this they put their face right behind and in line with the back of your skull which is the thicket and hardest part. Throwing your head back violently can easily break someone's nose or cheek. If they lean away the collar bone is accessible and breaks fairly easily when struck.

Figure 1

– Stomp their feet
 Lift your knee and slam the outside knife-edge of your foot or heel into the instep of their foot close to the leg bone. The intention is to break it.

– Kick their shins with your heels
 Blows to the shin are painful and can be disabling. If you get picked up, you can kick back with both feet.

– Groin strike and thigh pinch
 Sidestep, moving one foot to the side, let's say, your left foot. Then shift your hips over to the left. With your right hand, perform what we call a "hammer-fist" strike to the groin. This can be somewhat effective

in causing them to let go but don't stop there. With all four fingers of the same right hand, pinch their inner thigh, sometimes called a horse-bite. The right hand will always pinch their left thigh and vice versa. (Figure 2)

Figure 2

This thigh pinch is a very painful nerve strike that is used in law enforcement and self-defense training. In a SWAT instructor training seminar that I hosted, we ran a drill where one small group of guys had to forcibly take the larger group of guys out of a room using any method necessary as long as it didn't cause permanent injury. Guys were using pressure points, wrist locks, double-teaming and picking people up, dragging them by the ankles, etc. I was the last guy in the room doing my best to maneuver around attempts to constrain and move me until one "gentleman" said, "I'm tired of this," and grabbed my inner thigh from behind, turned and walked out of the room with me in tow totally compliant and in a lot of pain. It's a good move that usually causes people to respond quickly.

– Two-handed groin grab (reach back and squeeze)
Because the human body is approximately 65% water, it's fairly easy to maneuver your hands behind your hips, palms facing outward, and grab the attacker's groin area, that will line up perfectly, even if your hands are in front of you to start with. Picture moving your hands around so the backs of your hands are against your rear pockets. Then reach, grab and crush. (This doesn't work if your forearms are up and across your chest. If that happens, head-butt and stomp.)

If you are working in a care facility where you don't want to and are not allowed to hurt anyone and you find yourself in a bear hug, you can bring your hands to the rear then a little higher and tickle. This has been effective in causing people to let go because it's surprising and uncomfortable for them.

A word of warning: Once, while working as security in a nightclub, I put a guy who was very inebriated and disruptive in a perfect Aikido wrist lock to escort him out. In class, this particular wrist lock is amazingly painful and effective in controlling a person when applied right. I had him off balance and was walking him to the door when he looked at his wrist and then at me and said in a calm voice, "Why are you holding my arm?" I had him locked up pretty tight and this guy wasn't feeling a thing. Oops. Even though I was successful at removing him from the premises without further altercation, mainly because I had him mechanically out of balance, I learned a valuable lesson. Pain compliance techniques don't work very well with drunks; better have a plan B.

Rear Bear Hug (under the arms—elbows are not pinned)

Fighting responses include:

– Elbow strike to the face
Depending on exactly where you are being held and how tight, you may be able to twist and swing an elbow back into the attacker's face while holding their forearm with your other hand. Elbows are powerful weapons when thrown forcefully.

Other options include:

– Hitting the back of the attacker's hands (metacarpal bones)
The attacker's hands are in front of you and vulnerable. Hit the center of the bones with the second knuckle of your clenched fist. Hit as hard as you can; that goes without saying, right? Although these strikes do cause pain and can break the bones, this move is not your best single option.

– Grab fingers and rip them back, breaking them.
In a bear hug from behind, the attacker's hands and fingers are exposed and vulnerable. Grab a finger from the front, prying your fingers under theirs. Once you have one or two in your grasp don't hesitate to twist, bend and break them.

– Of course, kicking back into shins and feet is still a good option.

Front Bear Hug (Over the arms—arms pinned)

Fighting responses include:

– Yell in their ear
At 120 dB (decibels) the ear sustains immediate damage. Yelling in someone's ear at close range causes discomfort and usually a reactive pull back.

– Bite the neck and face

Biting causes severe trauma. In a front bear hug, you have, possibly, your best weapon in perfect range for maximum effectiveness. You can bite <u>anything</u> in range: face, neck, shoulder, etc.

- Head-butt to their face
  This is where you slam your forehead into the assailant's face. You have seen it a million times in movies but I'm betting you have never really considered using it. It's not a comfortable thought but the reason it's an option is because done right, it may be effective in causing enough pain and damage for the attacker to let go. This allows you precious time to escape or continue <u>your</u> counter-assault. The top of your forehead, right about at the hairline, is a very strong area of the skull. It makes a formidable weapon when striking the face or temple which has a much thinner and weaker bone structure. Strikes to the face can break bones, cause pain, the eyes to water and possibly stun momentarily. It takes a strong, committed strike.

- Stomp their feet

- Double hand groin grab
  Putting your open hands together palms facing your opponent, pinky fingers touching, allows you the opportunity to grab their groin and squeeze.

- Knee to the groin
  This is a powerful option anytime you are in close quarters facing the opponent. You can throw one or both knees continuously until you are free. This strike can be effective hitting the groin or the thighs. The way I teach it is to hit full force, not just to make contact but hard enough brake the pelvis. When you are in serious jeopardy you want to do maximum damage so they can't get up and pursue you as you escape.

Front Bear Hug (under arms—arms are free)

Fighting responses include:

You still have the knee strike, foot stomping, biting and head butting moves available but now, you can also use your hands and elbows.

– Palm Strike to side of the jaw has the potential to knock someone out.

– Eye Gouging (Figure 1)
   An eye gouge can be very effective from this frontal position where your hands are free. As described earlier; an eye gouge can be a good maneuver in foiling an attack and creating distance but a superior position is critical in deciding whether or not to use this move. If someone is sitting on top of you, you may not want to randomly poke the attacker in the eye as it could further his rage where he could start violently punching. However, that said, if you are fighting for your life, there are no rules and critics don't count.

– Elbow Striking (Figure 2)
   This is a strong move but takes some practice. I suggest hitting bags and targets to develop power and the confidence to throw this attack.

From a bear hug, you would lean back and violently bring your elbow across the assailant's jaw. I don't rely on a single move for success but a combination of moves. If one is not immediately effective, I move to a second and a third; biting, stomping, kneeing the groin, etc. In a low-level annoyance type bear hug, say at a party with friends, you could start with saying, "Let me go, RIGHT NOW!" Add big volume if he doesn't immediately comply. We don't always have to battle physically.

Figure 1   Figure 2

– Double Ear Clap
The ear strike, sometimes called clapping the ears, where you use the palm of one or both hands, to strike over the ears, can rupture the ear-drum, cause disorientation, pain, and even a knockout if it's done with sufficient force. As you strike the side of the head you may also impact the temple called (called the pterion, located just behind the zygomatic bone, where four skull bones meet.) Whether you strike the jaw, sternocleidomastoid muscle, temple or ear, all are considered good targets when things count. Needless to say, but I will again anyway, training, practice and more practice improves accuracy, power and overall competence. I encourage everyone to take the time to develop strong techniques and accuracy.

Voice Weapon

Your voice can do more than communicate a message through words and tone. At volume, it can serve to sound an alarm, startle or worse. At close range yelling in someone's ear can cause severe pain and damage the eardrum. Getting loud, suddenly, can trigger and the startle reflex ASR (acoustic startle response) that we all are susceptible to. It's part of our survival mechanism. At volumes over 80 dB (decibels) we, mostly unconsciously, react with a defense response. This event has serious undesirable effects on cognition (information processing). Simply put, when we are startled by a loud noise, we reactively jerk and tighten up. We are in a state of suspended animation for a second or more while we try and process the information and make sure we are still ok and uninjured and hopefully, moving toward safety.

In self-defense, we use this technique to startle an assailant to gain a moment to get clear of danger or gain an advantage. Imagine someone comes close to you and says quietly, "Do what I say and you won't get hurt." You suddenly scream at the top of your voice, "Get away from me!" and run, if possible. Screaming not only triggers a startle response but also releases a shot of adrenalin in you to aid your fight or flight. You disrupted their OODA loop. You are in charge of the action now, for a moment; capitalize on it.

Note of interest:

To maintain the element of surprise before going offensive on an attacker, never drop into a karate stance or boxer pose revealing that you have some training. Stealth and surprise are best. Catch the attacker with his defenses down. Practice a non-aggressive looking posture, with hands up, that, while appearing innocent actually sets you in a launch position for the double palm heel or your strike of choice.

Striking—Target Areas

In martial arts, we study several preferred areas on the human body to attack for maximum effectiveness. They include eyes, nose, groin, solar plexus, kidneys, base of the skull, temple, floating rib and so on. There is also an array of pressure points that we can exploit. With a little training, you can improve your accuracy, speed and power in hitting these areas. In this book, I will focus on the top few, most effective targets.

1. Mask area of the face
    A well-placed strike to the nose causes pain, injury, watery eyes and possible disorientation helping you to get clear. This area can be struck with several motions; a hammer-fist, open palm, front punch, elbow, knee, head butt or a kick. The hammer-fist uses the natural hitting motion that was discussed earlier.

2. Side of the jaw

The side of the jaw is an area that when hit right, with, let's say, a hook punch, can cause a knockout. I was sparring with a beginner student once. He turned around and covered up from my punches. I stopped, lowered my hands and started to turn around, disengaging. Just then he spun around and swung wildly, hitting me on the side of my jaw. He didn't have a lot of speed or power but the next thing I knew I was getting up off the floor. I was only unconscious for a second but that's all it takes to lose in the streets. Valuable lesson learned: a strike to the side of the jaw can render you unconscious. It's a prime real estate in boxing. It's a target that you definitely want to learn to protect. The primal block is one good way.

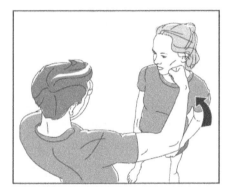

3. Eyes

You can use your fingers to pierce (strike) the eyes. This is different than the eye gouge. With your fingers extended in what we refer to as a spear hand position you make a quick, jabbing motion like throwing a punch but with an open hand. The striking point is the tip of the fingers. You know how unpleasant and distracting it is to have an eyelash or speck of dust in your eye. Imagine a finger punching into your eye socket. Of course, this move should only be used in extreme situations.

Knife-hand position

4. Shin
    Have you ever banged your shin into a coffee table? Hurts, right? Here
    are a few reasons why this is such a good target.

    • It's a large target area that stretches from your knee to the arch of
      your foot.
    • It's close to the ground so it's easier to maintain balance while
      striking.
    • It's almost impossible to block or move out of the way because you
      are standing upright and movement requires a weight shift which
      takes perception and time.
    • Evading a punch to the head by moving or blocking is much easier
      than trying to avoid a shin kick.

A good friend of mine, whom I'll call Jack, was walking with his girlfriend,
whom I will call Rachel, downtown, when two youths approached them.
One walked up to Jack and kicked him in the shin....totally unprovoked.
Jack immediately dropped to the ground in excruciating pain. The two
guys proceeded to push Rachel up against a building, dumped her purse
contents onto the ground, took what they wanted and then walked away.
She then walked over and helped Jack to his feet. They picked up the
remaining items and went home. Jack was a very fit, 25-year-old, strong
man at 6'2" and 200 pounds. He was also in martial arts at the time. He
was incapacitated by this one move. I have been hit with a shin kick at
different times. It's ridiculously painful and can be disabling for a time.

5. Groin

There are many good ways to attack this area including from behind. Kicking the groin is not as easy as it may seem. In the movies, they never miss—one simple kick and the bad guy collapses to the ground. He's incapacitated but not before bending over with legs together and flashing a surprised cross-eyed look at the camera. That's in the movies. Here are some things to consider: It's a relatively small target and it's a long way off the ground. The average adult male's groin area is at least 32 inches off the ground. There are large thigh muscles surrounding it and guys instinctively protect this area.

Having said that, the groin area is vulnerable from a few angles and useful in many instances. In close-quarter encounters, including front and rear bear hugs, and many grabbing situations, the groin can be hit with hands, knees or feet. In a rape situation, the groin is especially vulnerable to a possible biting or grabbing scenario. A friend of mine, was a first responder in a rape case where paramedics were called for a man who was hemorrhaging after he attempted to rape a woman. Yes, paramedics were called for a <u>man</u>, who was hemorrhaging after a failed rape attempt of a woman. She bit off his penis. The woman, or would-be rape victim, told the police, "Yeah, he put it where it didn't belong so I bit it off. I didn't have a problem with that." Police, tightening one corner of their mouths into a half grin and nodding to each other, were happy that she took charge and avoided being raped. She left a pretty impactful impression on the assailant also.

Another way of attacking the groin is to grab the testicles, then squeeze, twist and yank. Done right, it causes severe pain and trauma; as you might imagine. I know of one college student who used this move very successfully. Police showed up to find a guy traumatized on the floor.

6. Instep

Stomp on the instep of the assailant's foot to break it. Strike with the side knife-edge of your foot or the heel. It can be performed from the front, rear or side. If you are close, for instance, in a bear hug, this is a good fighting option. See figures 1 & 2.

Windup and stomp to the instep

7. Knee

Any kick to the knee can result in severe injury. Medial and lateral ligaments give way under very little pressure. The only problem is that the knee is rounded in front and slippery. In trying to deliver a front kick, you might miss or slip off because the profile of the foot, from that angle, is the thinnest. The sidekick is preferable if you can the positioning. Again, taking a martial arts class will improve your accuracy and the odds of landing these targeted attacks.

Chapter 10

GUNS

Should I carry a gun? Should I keep a gun in my house for personal safety? Am I prepared to use it and will I be effective with it when I need to be? All good questions. The answer is, it depends on your personal comfort level with firearms and your level of training. If you decide to purchase a firearm, do the research. Talk to people who sell guns and who own guns. Shoot different guns. Discover what option is right for you for home and carry. If you keep a firearm in your home, be sure to take precautions to prevent accidental misfires especially if you have children.

Type of Guns

There are several types of guns. Here are a few basics to consider in purchasing a gun for protection in the home.

Semi-automatic Pistol

The semi-automatic pistol (guns with a magazine that ejects for reloading) is the preferred firearm for military, law enforcement and personal carry mainly because of its high ammunition capacity and quick reloading capability. Reloading can be accomplished in split seconds where the revolver takes much longer. One drawback to this style of firearm is that it can jam (a round becomes lodged in the ejection port causing a malfunction). It can be cleared but that takes precious time.

Revolver

A revolver holds rounds (bullets) in a cylinder that rotates to bring a new round into firing position. These guns don't easily jam but only carry 5 or

6 shots and because of the round cylinder, they are usually bulkier than the semi-automatic pistols. They are not able to be reloaded quickly unless you carry quick loading equipment, which is unlikely.

Shooting accuracy is a function of barrel length and your skill level. Longer barrels give you greater accuracy but are harder to conceal if carrying.

Shotgun

A shotgun has been falsely labeled, in my opinion, as the best home and bedroom defense weapon. I disagree because:

1. It's big and heavy.
2. It's difficult to quickly change direction to hit multiple targets.
3. It takes time to rack in the next shell if it's a pump action.
4. The kick (the recoil) makes multiple shots on target difficult and can knock you off balance if you are in a less than ideal shooting posture.

Other Gun Considerations

For concealed carry, everyone has their personal preference; size, model, grip, caliber, round capacity, recoil, carry location on your body, holstering options, sights, optics and accessories are all factors. Talk to the experts. Try before you buy.

Ammunition for a pistol will depend on the caliber and barrel length of the gun. To be considered is penetration, expansion and muzzle velocity of the round (how fast the bullet is traveling as it exits the barrel). A good place to start for a 9mm pistol is Speer Gold Dot 124 grain, nickel-plated hollow point rounds. Or DPX 115 grain. Range ammunition will be different and less expensive.

For home and carry I use a 9 mm semi-automatic pistol. If I had unlimited funds, I think I would enjoy owning the AK-15 pistol. It's the preferred weapon of some experienced shooters.

Simi-automatic pistol   AR-15 Pistol 10.5-inch barrel

Revolver

Pump Shotgun

Shooting Position

The proper shooting stance helps stabilize your shot, perform multiple accurate hits on target, and maximize protection from incoming rounds (bullets coming at you). Depending on how you were taught and your success with one posture over another, you might have a stance preference. Also, different conditions and trains will demand flexibility in shooting techniques.

Stances

<u>Weaver Stance</u>

This stance was developed by Jack Weaver who was winning shooting competitions in the 1950s.) Some say this stance offers a stable platform and shooting control. It's more difficult for cross-eye dominant people (those who hold the gun in the right hand but sight through their left eye) and it exposes the vulnerable side of body armor.

<u>Isosceles Stance</u>

The isosceles stance is a forward-facing body position that presents the front plate of the body armor if you are wearing any. Weight is evenly distributed between your usually squared-off feet with both arms extended forward. From a top view, your chest and arms form an isosceles triangle, ergo the name. It is a stable stance that allows the bones of your arm and shoulder to absorb the recoil while offering some protection of your neck and head.

My preference is a modified, combat, forward aggressive, isosceles stance. It's a slightly bladed isosceles stance with one support leg more forward (left leg if you're right-handed). The shoulders are in front of the hips, weight on the balls of the feet, knees slightly bent. This aggressive, dynamic position allows greater mobility without losing armor protection. The more forward center-of-mass helps the shooter control recoil. Again, the gun, arms and hands provide some protection for the neck and face.

Center Axis Relock "CAR"

CAR was developed by Paul Castle— law enforcement officer and trainer. This canted, in close, comfortable grip makes it easier to focus on both the sights and target. It's good for weapon retention and maneuverability in close quarter battles. It also works well for cross-eye dominant shooters. Notice the tucked in elbows of both arms. This position is preferable because it offers less exposure to enemy combatants (bad guys) when clearing a room (slicing the pie) and also offers some protection from incoming rounds as opposed to a high, flagging elbow.

If you have seen the John Wick movies you will immediately recognize this shooting posture as Keanu Reeves character uses it frequently.

The proper grip is one important aspect of your stable shooting platform. By developing good technique through proper training, you can become comfortable and confident with your firearm whether you use it for practice and pleasure or personal protection.

Strong-side hand position

Off-side hand position

Whatever your weapon of choice and position of choice, be sure to get good training. There are a number of excellent firearms training centers in the U.S. with programs, taught by seasoned and professional law enforcement, military, and private citizen instructors, that go far beyond the basic CPL (concealed pistol license) course requirements: Front Site, Valor Ridge, TDI and Max Velocity to name just a few. Do some research as schools offer a variety of courses and areas of expertise ranging anywhere from personal and home protection to competition and marksman shooting, to tactical training for those who fight with guns. The cost of training also varies depending on the school and class level. Always practice responsible gun ownership and handling. Teach it to your kids. People get shot accidentally with "empty guns" all the time.

You can find many examples of the proper and improper use of firearms and we can learn from the experiences of others. I have included three stories here:

Growing up, I was taught never to point a gun at anything that I didn't intend to shoot. At age 17, I was working at the corner gas station. It had been robbed, at gunpoint, over the weekend so one employee decided to bring in a 16-gauge, pump shotgun, and leave it behind the counter, loaded. I'm working with another kid and I decided I didn't want a loaded gun sitting there so I picked it up and ejected "all" of the shells into a metal desk drawer. Then I aimed the gun at inanimate objects on the other side of a large glass window facing a busy street, and was thinking I should pull the trigger just to make sure it's not still cocked. It's ok, there are no bullets in the gun. But I didn't pull the trigger. Then, holding the gun off to the side of my co-worker only inches away, before putting the gun down, I purposely squeezed the trigger. ......
KABOOM! Shot pellets went through the metal wall, hit a compressor and bounced around the shop. My co-worker, a 16-year-old kid, fell backward and was sitting on the floor, shocked and eyes wide open, not saying a word. Holy cow, how did that happen? There was one round left in the chamber. I had emptied the bullets from the holding magazine but left one in firing position.

Peeping-Tom, Megan and a 357 Magnum

A few years ago, a lady whom I will call Megan and her husband lived next to a golf course in a small township. The couple didn't have kids but they did have a couple of good-sized dogs; one an Australian Shepard, the other a Collie mix. There wasn't much crime to speak of in this tiny little lakefront community but this week neighbors were talking about being frightened by a peeping tom. A peeping tom is someone who trespasses onto another's property to look in through a window or opening, violating a person's "reasonable expectation of privacy." They can also use mirrors, binoculars and cameras to peer through peepholes and windows without the consent of the person being viewed. Voyeurism, as this disorder is called, is usually done for sexual pleasure.

About midnight this particular evening, Megan was home alone enjoying a quiet evening. As she got up to move to another room, she caught sight of a dimly lit face peering in her window. Although startled and a little frightened, she didn't let on that she had seen the guy. What she did next is not recommended as it's illegal, but it was very effective. Megan walked into her bedroom and got her 357-magnum revolver. Then she called the dogs, walked to the front door and let them out. The dogs immediately went around the corner of the house and after the guy who was now high-tailing it off their property and across the golf course. Megan could see him running and, at this point, decided to send peeping-Tom a message. She aimed over his head and squeezed off the first round which was a 38-caliber bullet. Boom! The blast echoed off houses, breaking the quiet of the darkened sky. Then she squeezed off the second round, another 38-caliber bullet. The third and final shot was a 357-magnum round (a longer bullet holding more powder). The first two rounds were loud but the last shot was really loud - kaboom! - and threw fire 10 inches out the muzzle. There were no more incidents of peeping-Toms after that. Now, it's illegal to shoot a peeping-Tom who's running away, and it's not prudent to send lead, that will go over a mile, into the air, but it's still a cool story. Kind of badass. That was many years ago. Today you might find yourself in jail. Probably.

Downtown shooting

I remember when a well-known jewelry store in town was robbed. The thief had just grabbed a 19,000.00 Rolex watch and run out the door. The store owner grabbed his 38-caliber revolver, took off in pursuit and fired at the thief as he ran down the sidewalk. At least one bullet hit a bystander's car but no one was injured, and the thief got away. The store owner was charged with the reckless discharge of a firearm. The prosecutor commented that you have to take into consideration that your actions can endanger another person.

Gun safety rules to remember:

- All guns are always loaded
- Never point a gun at, or, sweep the muzzle of a gun past anything you don't intend to shoot
- Keep your fingers off of the trigger until you are ready to shoot
- Be sure of your target and what's behind it

Chapter 11
DEFUSE AND DE-ESCALATE

The ability to deescalate a situation helps us to manage aggressiveness and prevent escalation to violence. It's a sophisticated skillset as it requires us to be in total control of our own emotions while strategically applying de-escalating techniques to others, in high-stress situations.

In the chapter on acceptable use of force, surrounding circumstances including the possibility of alternative actions is considered when determining an appropriate and legal response. De-escalation is one of those possible alternative actions; if we have that tool in our toolbox. In other words; if we have a skill, we have the option of using it. If we don't, we don't.

Be Nice, Not Vulnerable

I read a great story years ago, I don't remember where, about a martial artist whom I'll call Steve, who was training in Japan. He had just received his black belt. He felt ready and confident to handle most any confrontation. He was riding the subway home and noticed a large, obnoxious guy who was obviously intoxicated, being loud and harassing passengers. Steve thought well, here we go. The guy got louder and more obnoxious so Steve rose to handle the situation. A chance to stand up for justice and what's right. A chance to use his training, he thought, "This guy was going down!" Just before he got to the man, an old gentleman sitting nearby reached out and took the drunk's arm and invited him to sit next to him. He did. The old man asked him what he had been drinking. He said nihonshu (saki). The old man said, "Ah, I like saki too." The wise old man, after establishing some rapport, lovingly and compassionately inquired as to his frustration. The man put his head on the old mans' shoulder and started crying. It turns out that his wife had just passed away and he felt angry, afraid and alone. Steve heard most of the conversation. Having been only seconds from pummeling this guy, puffing up his own ego,....... he sat down,..... ashamed. He was happy that no one else knew his intention.

It's better to defuse and avoid a fight if possible. Even if you are convinced that you are in the right and can beat the other person, it just takes one lucky punch to put you in the hospital with your jaw wired up or worse. Fighting may also result in some retaliatory aggression later where you are unprepared or outnumbered.

At a local night club and bowling alley, just a couple miles from my house, a security guard had asked a disruptive patron to leave the premises. Some angry words were exchanged and the guy left without further incident. An hour later the guy came back with a gun and shot the security guard in the face, killing him. One of my black belt students just happened to be in the parking lot and witnessed the killer's escape. Later the killer was caught, prosecuted and convicted of murder. Feeling disrespected, this guy was capable of vicious premeditated murder. You never know.

Another friend of mine was working security at a bar. He was an excellent martial artist and winner of a local Tough-Man contest. During his shift, he had to step in and stop a guy from pouring a beer on a pool table. The situation moved to the parking lot where the patron got aggressive and started a fight. My friend ended the fight with a spin hook kick to the side of the guy's head, knocking him out. The guy recovered and left with friends. The next night this same man came back with a shotgun. Luckily, my friend had the night off. The armed man left the premises without incident and didn't return.

Not everyone is a psychotic powder keg, one emotional spark away from going off. Angry people may be angry because they have had one too many frustrations, feel powerless or fearful. They've passed reason and now react. One compensatory view says, "Nothing suppresses a whimper better than a snarl." (author unknown). Because "angry men have no ears" it's important to help someone calm down in order to reason with them and see if their needs can be met; if you care. If you do, you have power.

In his book "Getting More", a book about how to successfully negotiate with people to succeed in work and life, Stuart Diamond states, "... emotions and perception are far more important than power and logic when dealing with others. Finding, valuing, and understanding the picture in their heads produce four times as much value as conventional tools like leverage and "win-win" because (a) you have a better starting point for persuasion, (b) people are more willing to do things for you when you value them, no matter who they are, and (c) the world is mostly about emotions, not the logic of "win-win." In short: The more you value others, the more they will value you.

(Getting More by Stewart Diamond, Copywrite © 2010, 2012, 2018 by Stewart Diamond. Published in the United States by Currency, an imprint of the Crown Publishing Group, division of Penguin Random House LLC, New York. ISBN 978-0-307-71691-0)

The most important skill in defusing anger is listening. Why? It shows that you are willing to take the time to understand. You value them and what they have to say. Here are some general rules in de-escalating hostility, according to research:

1. Communicate Respect
   • Show interest in resolving the issue and meeting needs
   • Acknowledge the importance of their concern
   • Refrain from judging their behavior

2. Cooperate
   • Do not disagree
   • Show empathy for the person's feelings

3. Effective Listening
   • Everyone wants to be listened to and feel understood
   • People get angry when they don't feel acknowledged for a long time
   • Paraphrase, clarify, gather more information
   • Validate the person's experience ("Yeah, I would probably feel the same way also if...")

- Use open-ended questions, e.g., "What would you like to see happen here?"
- Be aware of your reactions
- Attempt to turn judgment into curiosity ("Why do you think that is?")
- Stand at an angle, not directly opposing someone is a good non-adversarial position
- Use the person's name and don't talk too much
- Find what the person clearly values, e.g., "I can see that honesty and fairness are very important to you. They are to me as well."
- Find common ground

4. Reframing
   Reframing is a way to help someone look at situations from a different point of view. Some call this a paradigm shift.

   - One example is to redefine a problem as a challenge
   - Another would be to see challenges as opportunities to learn from for future success

5. Asserting - You can assert your own needs and interests to effectively manage the situation.
   - Set clear boundaries and expectations of appropriate behaviors
   - Be hard on issues but soft on the person
   - Use *I* statements not *you*. "*I* feel anxious when *you* pound the table; it makes it hard to listen to you."
   - Use 'and' statements rather than 'but.' "I see your point <u>and</u> I see the need for..."
   - Asserting may not be appropriate with a high -threat person

6. Disengaging - Remove yourself from a threatening situation when other methods are not working.
   - Explain the need for a break or a time out
   - Offer food or drink
   - Get assistance if possible

7. Losing it - When someone shows signs of losing control.
   • Get help before trouble starts
   • Stay calm—breathing techniques help
   • Talk slowly with a confident tone
   • Inform them of inappropriate behavior
   • Leave yourself an escape route
   • Debrief with others, staff, supervisors, if necessary

One of my students came to me at age seventeen wanting to be a police officer. He became a cop and went on to become head of the SWAT team and then detective. His advice to de-escalate hostility, initially, is: say "I'm sorry." It's disarming.

Classic De-escalation Story

I was at an Olympic qualifying karate tournament in West Virginia. The venue, a gymnasium, was designed with the spectator seating in a balcony overlooking the playing surface. All the competitors were warming up on the gymnasium floor getting ready for their sparring matches. No one was allowed on the main level except competitors. In many other similar events, held throughout the year, parents and coaches are allowed to be closer to ringside to take pictures and cheer on the kids. This was a very professional event, so much so, that every ring's corner judges were wearing tuxedos.

Just before the competition, I heard a woman shouting at an official, demanding to be able to stand ringside to video her son. No other parent or coach was allowed to be there but this very imposing, nearly hysterical woman was not going to cooperate. I stepped closer to assist. Just then, a man who was helping coordinate the event took charge. I was thinking that he was going to say something like, "I'm sorry ma'am but no one is allowed in this area, except competitors, and if we make an exception for you, we would have to allow everyone…" Or "Excuse me ma'am, you are holding up this entire event and you will need to go to the seating area where you can see this ring just fine and take your pictures from there." This gentleman did something different and brilliant. He introduced himself and then asked, "What is your concern?" She said "I want to take pictures. I came a long way and I'm going to take pictures of my son competing." He said, "Oh yes, I understand. That is important. Your son is competing in this ring here?" Yes. "Would it be ok if I filmed the match for you? I'm very qualified with a video camera." I was thinking oh, this woman is going to have no part of that suggestion. To my surprise, she said "Yes, thank you, that would be fine." What had the makings of a hot mess of disruption and confrontation, with a paid guest being furious, was resolved and all were happy. I learned a valuable lesson.

I'm no expert on the Bible but it offers a couple of ideas that might be valuable to us here. It states:

"...let every man be swift to hear, slow to speak, slow to wrath (James 1:19 Scripture taken from the New King James Version®. Copyright © 1982 by Thomas Nelson. Used by permission. All rights reserved.

"He who is slow to anger is better than the mighty,.." Prov. 16:32 NKJV Bible Scripture taken from the New King James Version®. Copyright © 1982 by Thomas Nelson. Used by permission. All rights reserved.)

Let's try gentle words and deescalate the whole matter if we can.

It is better to avoid danger than get out of danger. It's better to be patient rather than hot-tempered. A good self-defense arsenal needs to include kindness and de-escalation skills.

Chapter 12

LIVE YOUR LIFE AND BE SAFE

No one stays in one spot. We move around and experience life. Take steps to be safe.

Car Smart

While driving, if you believe you are being followed, remember the rule of four turns. Turn right four times. If the vehicle is still behind you, drive to a police station or busy gas station. Alert others that you are being followed. Make note of the make, model and color of the car, number of passengers and license plate number. Identification of a suspect vehicle is easy during the day. At night it's harder, but you can note the headlight pattern, bulb brightness, number of passengers backlit from other traffic, etc. Never drive home if you suspect you are being followed. Do not exit your vehicle unless the surroundings are safe.

Your car is a superior weapon

The average car weighs 1.5 tons and the average SUV 2.5 tons. It has locks, lights, a horn, maybe a dash-cam, and it can accelerate to move you away from danger. If you are being blocked by a riotous crowd, you can drive slowly moving people out of the way.

Safe distance

When driving, make sure you have a two-second gap between you and the next car in front of you, at any speed you may be traveling. Watch as the car in front of you passes an object: a tree, pole, sign, anything. Count one-one-thousand, two-one-thousand and you should pass it. Less than that and you reduce reaction time in avoiding a collision should that car stop unexpectedly.

At a traffic light, stay back a car length or far enough that you can see the bottom of the rear tires of the car in front of you. If you need to escape, you have the room to pull forward and out. This prevents you from being boxed in.

Never tailgate. End of story. Drive defensively giving yourself options if you need to change lanes quickly or stop in poor road conditions. I have learned not to road rage and be reckless with an automobile in my hands. You can too. Do some deep breathing and relax. You know you are going to be cut off in traffic. Accept it. Back off and reestablish your safety gap. Yes, others will jump in front of you filling that space. Expect it, accept it. A couple of minutes extra in arriving at your destination is not worth the stress and risk of reckless driving.

The Bump and Run (Carjacking)

The Bump and Run is one of the most common forms of carjacking and robbery. Someone bumps your car's rear bumper while you are at a stop. You are an honest person wanting to do the right thing. You know you are in the right so you get out to exchange information. The perp pulls a weapon and tells you to lay on the ground, robs you, then takes your car or you and your car. First thing: Never get out of your car if you feel unsafe. Trust your instincts. You can exchange information through a cracked window. You are also completely within your rights to inform the other driver that you are going to drive to a more lighted more populated area because you think this area is unsafe. If this is an honest person, they will have no problem with your concerns. If their intentions are nefarious, they will protest and probably drive away. You just saved yourself. You can drive away, call 911 and give them a description.

The Elevator

A woman is in an elevator. The doors open and a man steps in. The doors close. He turns to her and says, "Don't resist and I won't have to hurt you." He moves closer. She says, "Oh, you've got this all wrong. You are going to be the one hurting." She, having trained in martial arts, was prepared. When the doors finally opened, witnesses said he was screaming for someone to get her off of him. She pummeled him to the floor and didn't stop there. There are some pretty interesting security camera videos depicting women defending themselves in elevators, if you want to see them for yourself. These women weren't afraid to fight against inappropriate conduct. Check them out.

<u>Preemptive moves</u>

The elevator doors open and a suspicious character steps in. Before the doors close you decide to step off and take the next elevator.

Your position once in an elevator should always be by the control panel if possible. Locate the emergency alarm and know how to activate it. Also, keep your back to the walls and don't let people get behind you if you can help it.

Before boarding the elevator, be sure you know what direction it's heading. You don't want to take an unwanted ride to the basement. Be aware of who is in the elevator or who is getting on and be willing to step off and take the stairs or the next ride.

Safety on The Street

There are things you can do to minimize your risk of assault while in public. When walking on the sidewalk, walk facing oncoming traffic. It allows you to see a vehicle slowing or stopping near you. Someone can't surprise you by approaching you from behind.

Yes, you say, that makes sense, but who is actually going to take the time to cross to the other side of the street so they can walk facing traffic? The real question is: Do I want to take the time and isn't that being a little paranoid? The truth is that knowing our potential vulnerabilities and taking reasonable precautions is prudent and it does take a little time but only a couple seconds. You are worth those couple seconds.

In "How to Be Your Own Bodyguard" author Nick Hughes gives an example of the two-second rule. He describes one of the biggest massacres in this country that happened at a well-known fast-food restaurant in Texas in the 1980's. A man that had worked as a welder, walked into the restaurant, armed to the teeth, completely intent on killing everyone inside. He used an Uzi, a shotgun and handgun to kill 21 victims and injure 15 more people before being shot by a SWAT sniper from a nearby rooftop. If you'd been inside and able to see the door, and saw someone approaching with weapons, says Nick, that may have given you sufficient advance knowledge to either leave the premises or draw your own weapon and get ready to engage them. If, on the other hand, your back was to the door, the first time you'd have known about it is when you were either shot in the back of the head or ordered onto the ground to be killed, execution style. How much longer does it take to sit facing the door? About two seconds. Hughes explains, "the return on that tiny investment of only two seconds of time is absolutely huge. For men, this means going into a stall in a public restroom instead of standing at a urinal, two seconds extra. Putting on a seat-belt, two seconds. Putting on boots or lace up shoes instead of flip flops two seconds. Taking your weapon with you instead of leaving it at home, two seconds. Taking the time to be prepared takes very little extra time compared to not being prepared, but the payoff is vast." Like I said earlier; I always sit facing the door when in a restaurant.

(How to Be Your Own Bodyguard by Nicholas Hughes. Copywrite © 2017 by Nicholas Hughes, Warriors Krav Maga Print Edition: ISBN 97809856519)

So, if possible, walk facing traffic and not too close to the road so a vehicle can't easily roll up close behind you without you noticing. A woman, who had taken my self-defense class, just a month earlier, was walking alone on the sidewalk near a fairly busy street. She was walking with the traffic flow. A car pulled up next to her. The door opened, a guy rushed out, grabbed her arm and pulled her toward the car. She was startled but her training kicked in. She stepped into the pull, regained her balance and launched a perfect sidekick to his knee. She said that all she heard, after the loud pop, of a probably dislocated knee, as she ran away, was, "Ooooh....my leg!" She said there were three guys in the car. Wow, too close. Another example of someone taking the time to prepare for a potential assault and then executing.

Travel Tips

Before heading out into the world, research travel safety tips for that area. Consider these:

1. Make sure your baggage is easily identifiable and that you handle your own baggage.
2. Don't let your bags out of sight for a second.
3. Don't accept cab rides whose rates seem too good to be true. Go with reputable companies that display the driver's medallion number (NYC permit) or license.
4. Stay in well-populated areas and well-lit areas at night.
5. Map out your route and know where you are going.
6. Know how subways work. Stand behind the yellow line on the platform while waiting. Know transportation options and systems for your destination.
7. There are predators waiting for unsuspecting, unsophisticated travelers. Women, to protect from purse snatching, wear your purse strap across your body with your purse under your arm. Men, avoid carrying wallets in the back pocket. Pickpockets can work in teams. One causes a disturbance while the others relieve you of your valuables.

8. The best way to refuse a street panhandler is to say "Sorry." and keep moving.

9. Watch your drinking and never leave your drink unattended. Get them only from the bartender.

10. Blend in as much as possible when abroad. Be careful wearing shorts, sleeveless shirts or flip-flops in Europe, especially, France and Italy. Doing so, showing too much skin, may be considered disrespectful, and you'll immediately be spotted as a tourist. In St. Peter's Basilica, and the cathedrals of Florence, Siena and Lucca there is a dress code against showing knees and shoulders. And even if they don't always strictly enforce the dress code due to very hot weather, for example, you'll be looked upon with disdain. We want to be polite guests respecting another countries heritage and traditions when traveling. We want to represent ourselves and our country well. (my opinion)

11. Project confidence, or, the appearance of confidence and vigilance

12. Buy travel insurance.

13. Don't trust easily.

14. Statistics show that 110 million people used Uber's ride-sharing app on a monthly basis in late 2019, pre-Covid, and 55 million users in mid-2020 during Covid (Covid-19 pandemic period). Ride-hauling companies Uber and Lyft released frightening statistics on the perils of using their services in regard to sexual assaults, fatalities related to Uber trips and murders. As the industry rushes to introduce more safety features to protect their clients, we have to do what we can to protect ourselves. Uber offers a safety tip list on their web site. I suggest you take the time to read it. The following is an example of what's on that list.

    a. Request your ride inside.
    Minimize the time that you're standing outside by yourself with your phone in your hand. Instead, wait inside until the app shows that your driver has arrived.

    b. Check your ride matching the license plate, car make and model, and driver photo with what's provided in your app.

    c. Have the driver confirm your name: Ask "Who are you here to pick up?"

d. Ride in the back-seat for easy exit on either side of the vehicle if escape becomes necessary.

e. While in route, tap share trip status in the app to share your driver's name, photo, license plate, and location with a friend or family member. They will receive a text or push notification that tracks your trip and ETA.

f. If you ever feel that you're in an urgent situation, you can call 911 by using the Emergency Button located in your app.

My two sons, Erik-age 21 and Alex-age 18, at the time, went on the trip of a lifetime across Africa. They bought travel insurance and moved through 9 countries on motorcycles, taking 3.5 months. They ran into some trouble (an understatement) near the end of their journey in Cairo, Egypt. Their travel and extraction insurance was one of the things that contributed to saving my son's life. It's not a joke when you need it. I suggest you buy it when traveling. I won't go into the amazing adventures and the horrific challenges that these two courageous kids faced, along with their two friends, but it's a story well worth reading, "The Only Road North" by Erik Mirandette.

Beware—Poison in Your Drink

Beware; while you're not looking someone is putting a powerful poison in your drink that causes loss of all control, and comatose conditions. You are being raped; you can't stop it and you won't be able to recall it. Beware. Don't let this be you.

Drug Facilitated Sexual Assault (DFSA)

Or by another definition: Incapacitated, non-consensual, drug-facilitated sexual assault perpetrated by socially inept, limp-dick, opportunistic, self-absorbed A**-hole, losers…. In my opinion.

According to the latest research and cross-disciplinary studies, GHB (Gamma Hydroxybutyric Acid, street name Easy Lay and Liquid X) and Rohypnol, (generic name Flunitrazepam, street name Roofie) are date-rape drugs. They are strong hypnotic depressants, Flunitrazepam being ten times more potent than diazepam (Valium).

Until recently, these drugs, one a liquid the other in solid pill form, were odorless, tasteless and colorless. Today Rohypnol is a green pill with a blue core that turns liquids blue so it's not as easy to slip into a drink unnoticed anymore. A small amount, as little as one mg, can impair an individual for 8 to 12 hours. Among its effects are drowsiness, forgetfulness to amnesia, seizure-like loss of muscle control, coma and loss of inhibitions. This makes fighting off a sexual predator or rapist impossible and because it affects memory it's hard to press charges for things you don't remember on people you can't identify. Toxicology of these poisons is difficult in such small amounts and also because they dissipate from the bloodstream within a few hours.

Who can you trust? Bill Cosby, America's quintessential tv dad, is a serial rapist who drugged and violated untold numbers of women. Trust takes time. It's earned. Don't trust easily. Guard your drink and your friend's drink.

Here is a good list that the U.S. Department of Justice, Drug Enforcement Agency (USDOJ-DEA) offers to the public that gives you guidelines to protect yourself and what to do if you suspect you have been drugged or assaulted. I decided to include the list in its entirety.

Protect Yourself

- Don't drink from a can or bottle that **you didn't open yourself**
- Don't take a drink from a **punch bowl**
- Don't drink from a container that's being passed around
- If someone offers you a drink from the bar at a club or party, don't take it. Instead, go to the bar to **order your own drink**, watch it being poured, and carry the drink yourself.
- Don't **leave your drink unattended** while talking, dancing, using the restroom or making a phone call
- If you realize that your drink has been left unattended, **throw it out** and get a new one
- Don't drink anything that has an unusual taste or appearance; like a **salty taste** or unexplained residue

111

- Don't **mix drugs and alcohol**. Even over-the-counter drugs like cold medicine can react with alcohol and other substances in negative ways.
- **Watch out for your friends** and ask them to watch out for you
- Have a plan to periodically check up on each other
- If your friend appears very intoxicated, gets sick after drinking a beverage, passes out and is difficult to wake up, seems to have trouble breathing or behaves in unusual ways, do what you need to do to make sure your friend is safe. **Call 911** if necessary.

Signs That You May Have Been Drugged

- You feel drunk even though you haven't had alcohol
- You wake up very hungover and have a memory lapse or can't account for a period of time
- Your clothes are a mess or not on right
- You are nauseous, sleepy and have a loss of reflexes
- You feel like someone had sex with you but you can't remember it

What to Do

What should you do if your drink was drugged and you think you've been sexually assaulted?

1. Go to a safe place. Ask a trusted friend to stay with you.
2. Call the police. Tell the police everything. Be honest about your activities. Remember that nothing justifies sexual assault.
3. Go to a hospital as soon as possible. Ask for an exam and evidence collection. Request that the hospital take a urine sample for drug toxicology testing. Have them test for GHB, Rohypnol, Ecstasy and Ketamine.
4. Preserve as much physical evidence as possible. Don't bathe, shower or throw away clothing you were wearing during the incident until you've talked to the police and been examined by a doctor. Save any other potential evidence, like the glass that held your drink.
5. Call a sexual assault crisis center for support and information.

Chapter 13

INTIMATE PARTNER ABUSE

I had known Sandy for a couple years and she knew that I taught self-defense. One day I noticed a bruise on her face and asked her about it. She was willing to open up a little and said it was from her live-in boyfriend. She said he didn't hit her often but because she loved him, she was not ready to leave him. Later she asked me for some pepper spray because he would get drunk, come in late at night and threaten her. I supplied her with a 68-shot canister of pepper spray. Two days later she called and asked for another one. I assumed that she lost it. She said, "No. I used it up. He came in at night, drunk and said he was going to kill me. He had a knife. I sprayed him in the face as he came down the hallway towards the bedroom. I kept spraying him in the face until he crawled out the front door, down the steps and onto the grass where he crawled in circles until the police showed up." She still didn't leave him because she loved him and wanted to give him another chance, or that's what she told me. Unfortunately, because of the Stockholm syndrome, feelings of inferiority, the perceived dangers of escape and other factors, including feeling a lack of realistic, good options, many women stay with their abusive partners too long. Then Sandy got pregnant. A few months later she told me that she had left him, finally. I congratulated her and asked how she got the courage to leave. She said, "her man" got angry while they were driving somewhere. He reached over, opened the door and kicked her out of the moving car. (shocking right?) "It was now about more than just me.", she explained. Today Sandy and her daughter are doing well.

Alice and I had a mutual friend named June. June, myself, and others, were getting together for a quick coffee after work so I invited Alice to come along. She said she was not able to because her husband would be too upset. I suggested he come along too but she said he would never do that and if she was even a few minutes late getting home after work, he would interrogate her to find out exactly where she was. She had to go directly home after work and even report to him if she stopped to get gas. I was shocked. It disgusted me that she was a prisoner in her life. As a friend, I suggested that she may want to reconsider the relationship as she had only been married a couple years and had no children. I recommended that she seek help with a local agency and get counseling. Over a short period of time, he became increasingly more possessive and abusive. One evening he got outraged and chased her around the yard with his Jeep. She then, decided to leave him. Fortunately, he didn't harass or stalk her after the breakup. The restraining order probably helped. I'm being sarcastic. The restraining order helped.

According to the National Coalition Against Domestic Violence (NCADV, NCADV.org):

- On a typical day, there are more than 20,000 phone calls placed to domestic violence hotlines nationwide
- Intimate partner violence accounts for 15% of all violent crime
- Women between the ages of 18-24 are most commonly abused by an intimate partner

How long do you wait?

The following story is about a lovely, strong woman who, having marital problems, let her husband know she was considering leaving him. She didn't believe that he would escalate beyond the violence she had already known; especially with the kids around.Of course, I share this story with you in hopes that you will never be in any circumstance close to this.

My good friend, whom I'll call Marty, was devastated by the news. His wonderful friend, whom I'll call Sarah, didn't show up to work one beautiful spring morning. Just the night before, Sarah's girlfriend called to check on her. Sarah told her that she was fine and that her husband wouldn't do anything while the kids are home. But there was talk. Even though she didn't bring her private life to work, those close to Sarah knew she was having marital difficulties and were worried for her. Her boss and coworkers all said that she was a one-of-a kind, someone who made people around her better, a woman full of life and love. The next paragraph is graphic and so very sad.

One early morning in April, as Sarah was lying in their bed with one of their young children, her husband walked into the room with a gun. He raised the gun toward Sarah and shot her. Sarah ran and was shot several more times killing her. Her husband was later found, by one of the children, in the basement, dead, with a self-inflicted gunshot wound to the head.

A month earlier Sarah had posted on social media that she was looking for another place to live. It seems she was considering leaving her husband. He was not going to let that happen.

As a cancer survivor, diagnosed when her youngest child was only very young, she worked to support local charities to help others. She survived a broken neck that she received earlier in her life in a car accident; and then this wonderful lady's life was ended by her husband. Her plan and timing didn't afford her a realistic escape considering the extent of his obsessive, control issues and mental state. Her children are growing up without their parents.

Please do not tolerate or take abuse lightly. Do some research on the warning signs of an abusive relationship. There are state and national domestic violence hotlines that you can call to get immediate assistance. There are safe houses available, supported by community charitable groups, that will house you and your children and help you relocate anonymously. It's important, although not easy, to make a plan. Discover your resources and options. DO NOT discuss it with your spouse or partner. No one can intervene and advocate for you better than you. Your life is precious. Don't wait too long.

Chapter 14

10 COMMANDMENTS OF PERSONAL SAFETY

Here are my 10 commandments for personal safety. Embracing any or all of these protective measures will reduce your risk of becoming a victim and increase your personal power.

1. I will not be bullied, coerced, or intimidated.
2. I will set and enforce boundaries verbally, physically and emotionally.
3. I will plan ahead, minimize risk, and use safe practices.
4. I have a right to self-defense and can use force if I choose to.
5. I will continuously train, improve my skills and be a hard target.
6. I will be vigilant.
7. I will not increase vulnerability by being impaired or incapacitated with drugs and alcohol.
8. I will project confidence in public. I will fake it if I don't always feel it.
9. I will not trust easily. Trust is earned. It takes time. I'm worth it. Get over it.
10. I will know the way out, defuse aggression if possible and use force as a last resort. But I will go to war if necessary.

Knowledge, preparation and courage all lead to one objective: victory.

We need to be victorious because without it nothing else matters.

CONGRATULATIONS

Congratulations, you made it through the book. Hopefully, you can now, with the knowledge you've gained, do things differently. You can change blind spots to strong points. Although this book addresses uncomfortable realities, it's not meant to dissuade you from boldly living your life, your one and only life, to the fullest.

As one author put it:

"The most horrible and terrifying thing that I can imagine isn't that I would put all that I am on the line for a cause I believe in and then be called on it. The most horrible and terrifying thing is the thought that I could spend my whole existence minimizing the risks I take, living ignorantly convinced of my safety, rejecting the purpose I was created for, and then someday wake up an old man and see that my life has passed before me, and now with death knocking on my door realize that in all my years I have never truly lived." Erik Mirandette, The Only Road North.

Taken from "The Only Road North" by Erik Mirandette – Copyright © 2007, by Erik Mirandette. Used by permission of Zondervan. www.zondevan.com

Everyone dies. Not everyone really lives. So, my wish for you is to struggle well and live-out-loud. As George Eliot says, "It's never too late to be all you might have been." Take risks and be bold. That doesn't mean to be reckless.

What are you prepared to do?

Victories await.

Rick Mirandette